The Diver Returns

Circular Functions, Vector Components, and Complex Numbers

Teacher's Guide

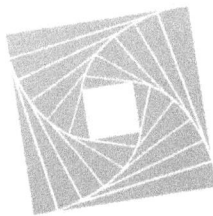

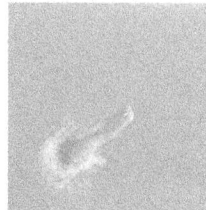

This material is based upon work supported by the National Science Foundation under award numbers ESI-9255262, ESI-0137805, and ESI-0627821. Any opinions, findings, and conclusions or recommendations expressed in this publication are those of the authors and do not necessarily reflect the views of the National Science Foundation.

Key Curriculum
1150 65th Street
Emeryville, California 94608
email: editorial@keypress.com
www.keycurriculum.com

First Edition Authors

Dan Fendel, Diane Resek, Lynne Alper, and Sherry Fraser

Contributors to the Second Edition

Sherry Fraser, Jean Klanica, Brian Lawler, Eric Robinson, Lew Romagnano, Rick Marks, Dan Brutlag, Alan Olds, Mike Bryant, Jeri P. Philbrick, Lori Green, Matt Bremer, Margaret DeArmond

Editor

Mali Apple

Editorial Assistant

Emily Reed

Professional Reviewer

Rick Marks, Sonoma State University

Math Checker

Carrie Gongaware

Production Editor

Andrew Jones

Production Director

Christine Osborne

Executive Editor

Josephine Noah

Mathematics Product Manager

Elizabeth DeCarli

Publisher

Steven Rasmussen

Contents

Blackline Masters

Calculator Guide and Calculator Notes

Introduction

The Diver Returns Unit Overview

Intent

This unit follows up on the ideas from the final Year 3 unit, *High Dive,* which concerns a circus act in which a diver is dropped from a turning Ferris wheel into a tub of water carried by a moving cart. The basic problem is to determine when his fall should begin in order for the diver to land in the water.

Mathematics

This unit uses key ideas from *High Dive,* including the extension of the trigonometric functions and the physics of objects falling from rest. The unit builds on those ideas, especially extending the physics principles to include motion with both horizontal and vertical initial components, which students learn to express as vectors. This leads to a study of quadratic equations and the need to express a solution in terms of the coefficients. That work culminates in the development of the quadratic formula and an introduction of complex numbers.

The main concepts and skills that students will encounter and practice during the unit are summarized below.

Trigonometry and Geometry
- Using the extended trigonometric functions
- Applying the principle that the tangent to a circle is perpendicular to the radius at the point of tangency

Physics
- Reinforcing the idea that a person falling from a moving object will follow a different path than someone falling from a stationary object
- Expressing velocity in terms of vertical and horizontal components
- Representing the motion of falling objects when the vertical and horizontal components of the initial velocity are both nonzero

Quadratic Equations
- Recognizing the importance of quadratic equations in the analysis of falling objects
- Developing the quadratic formula
- Using the quadratic formula to solve quadratic equations
- Finding a general solution for the falling time of objects with an initial vertical velocity

Complex Numbers
- Seeing the need to extend the number system to solve certain quadratic equations
- Establishing basic ideas about complex number arithmetic
- Representing complex numbers in the plane and seeing addition of complex numbers as a vector sum

Progression

In *High Dive,* students simplified the unit problem by assuming that the diver fell as if from a stationary platform. In this unit, students begin with a review of the key ideas of that simplified problem, including the extension of the trigonometric functions of sine and cosine beyond the right-triangle context and the physics of objects moving with constant acceleration, as in gravitational fall.

Students then look at the initial velocity given to the diver through the turning of the Ferris wheel. They examine how an initial vertical component of velocity, either upward or downward, changes the diver's falling time. They see that finding the falling time requires solving a quadratic equation, which leads to an excursion into the quadratic formula.

Students also must grapple with the task of determining both the vertical and horizontal components of the diver's initial velocity, and they must determine how the horizontal component of his initial velocity affects where he lands. The issues related to finding the separate components are dealt with in a series of paired problems, with one problem in each pair involving the Ferris wheel situation and the other set in another context. Students develop a general expression, based on the physical context, for the time it takes a falling object to reach the ground, in terms of its initial height and vertical velocity.

Finally, students return to the circus act problem in its full complexity. They combine their formula for falling time with expressions for the vertical and horizontal components of the diver's velocity. This leads to a very complex expression for the diver's position when he is about to land, in terms of the time of his release from the Ferris wheel. Comparing this with the position of the moving cart leads to an equation that will solve the problem. This equation is solved graphically.

Back to the Circus: Reviewing the simplified problem from *High Dive* and the concepts involved in solving that problem

A Falling Start: Analyzing the height and falling time for falling objects with nonzero initial vertical velocity, with a digression on the quadratic formula

Components of Velocity: Separating velocity into vertical and horizontal components, and analyzing these components for the diver in the unit problem

The Diver Really Returns: Solving the unit problem, a digression about the complex plane, and compiling portfolios

Pacing Guides

50-minute Pacing Guide (22 days)

Day	Activity	In-Class Time Estimate
	Back to the Circus	5
	The Circus Act	5
	Homework: As the Ferris Wheel Turns	0
2	Discussion: As the Ferris Wheel Turns	50
	Homework: Graphing the Ferris Wheel	0
3	Discussion: Graphing the Ferris Wheel	10
	Distance with Changing Speed	30
	Homework: Free Fall	10
4	Discussion: Free Fall	15
	Moving Cart, Turning Ferris Wheel	35
	Homework: Moving Cart, Turning Ferris Wheel (continued)	0
5	Moving Cart, Turning Ferris Wheel (continued)	30
	Introduce: POW 1: Which Weights Weigh What?	10
	Introduce: Reference: The Standard POW Write-up	0
	Homework: A Simple Summary and a Complex Beginning	10
6	Discussion: A Simple Summary and a Complex Beginning	20
	A Falling Start	0
	Look Out Below!	30
	Homework: The Diver and the POW	0
7	Discussion: The Diver and the POW	15
	Look Out Below! (continued)	35
	Homework: Big Push	0
8	Discussion: Big Push	10
	Finding with the Formula	40
	Homework: Using Your ABC's	0
9	Discussion: Using Your ABC's	20
	Imagine a Solution	30
	Homework: Complex Numbers and Quadratic Equations	0

10	Discussion: Complex Numbers and Quadratic Equations	10
	Complex Components	30
	Homework: Three O'Clock Drop	10
11	Discussion: Three O'Clock Drop	20
	Up, Down, Splat!	25
	Homework: Falling Time for Vertical Motion	5
12	Discussion: Falling Time for Vertical Motion	15
	Components of Velocity	0
	High Noon	35
	Homework: Leap of Faith	0
13	Discussion: Leap of Faith	10
	High Noon (continued)	5
	The Ideal Skateboard	35
	Homework: Racing the River	0
14	Discussion: Racing the River	10
	The Ideal Skateboard (continued)	15
	One O'Clock Without Gravity	25
	Homework: Swimming Pointers	0
15	One O'Clock Without Gravity (continued)	10
	Discussion: Swimming Pointers	10
	Vector Velocities	30
	Homework: Velocities on the Wheel	0
16	Discussion: Velocities on the Wheel	20
	Release at Any Angle	30
	Homework: An Expanded Portfolio of Formulas	0
17	Discussion: An Expanded Portfolio of Formulas	10
	Moving Diver at Two O'Clock	40
	Homework: The Danger of Simplification	0
18	Discussion: The Danger of Simplification	20
	The Diver Really Returns	0
	The Diver's Success	30
	Homework: A Circus Reflection	0
19	Discussion: A Circus Reflection	z
	The Diver's Success (continued)	35
	Homework: Beginning Portfolio Selection	5

20	Presentations: POW 1: Which Weights Weigh What?	35
	Homework: "The Diver Returns" Portfolio (begin in class)	15
21	In-Class Assessment	50
	Homework: Take-Home Assessment	0
22	Exam Discussion	35
	Unit Reflection	15

90-minute Pacing Guide (15 days)

Day	Activity	In-Class Time Estimate
1	Back to the Circus	0
	The Circus Act	45
	As the Ferris Wheel Turns	35
	Homework: Distance with Changing Speed	10
2	As the Ferris Wheel Turns (continued)	40
	Discussion: Distance with Changing Speed	10
	Free Fall	40
	Homework: Graphing the Ferris Wheel	0
3	Discussion: Graphing the Ferris Wheel	15
	Free Fall (continued)	20
	Moving Cart, Turning Ferris Wheel	45
	Homework: A Simple Summary and a Complex Beginning	10
4	Moving Cart, Turning Ferris Wheel (continued)	20
	Discussion: A Simple Summary and a Complex Beginning	20
	Introduce: POW 1: Which Weights Weigh What?	15
	Introduce Reference: The Standard POW Write-up	5
	A Falling Start	0
	Look Out Below!	30
	Homework: The Diver and the POW	0
5	Discussion: The Diver and the POW	15
	Look Out Below! (continued)	25
	Big Push	35
	Homework: Finding with the Formula	15
6	Discussion: Finding with the Formula	10
	Using Your ABC's	50
	Imagine a Solution	30
	Homework: Complex Numbers and Quadratic Equations	0
7	Discussion: Complex Numbers and Quadratic Equations	15
	Complex Components	30

	Three O'Clock Drop	45
	Homework: Up, Down, Splat!	0
8	Discussion: Up, Down, Splat!	15
	Falling Time for Vertical Motion	35
	Components of Velocity	0
	High Noon	40
	Homework: Leap of Faith	0
9	Discussion: Leap of Faith	10
	The Ideal Skateboard	40
	Racing the River	40
	Homework: One O'Clock Without Gravity	0
10	Discussion: One O'Clock Without Gravity	10
	Swimming Pointers	25
	Vector Velocities	40
	Homework: Velocities on the Wheel (begin in class)	15
11	Discussion: Velocities on the Wheel	15
	Release at Any Angle	35
	Moving Diver at Two O'Clock	40
	Homework: An Expanded Portfolio of Formulas	0
12	Discussion: An Expanded Portfolio of Formulas	15
	The Danger of Simplification	45
	The Diver Really Returns	0
	The Diver's Success	30
	Homework: A Circus Reflection	0
13	Discussion: A Circus Reflection	10
	The Diver's Success (continued)	35
	Homework: Beginning Portfolio Selection and "The Diver Returns" Portfolio (begin in class)	35
14	Presentations: POW 1: Which Weights Weigh What?	35
	In-Class Assessment	40
	Take-Home Assessment (begin in class)	15
15	Exam Discussion	45
	Unit Reflection	20

Materials and Supplies

All IMP classrooms should have a set of standard supplies, described in the section "Materials and Supplies for the IMP Classroom" in A Guide to IMP. You'll also find a comprehensive list of materials needed for all Year 4 units in the section "Materials and Supplies for Year 4" in the Year 4 Teacher's Guide general resources.

Listed here are the supplies needed for this unit. Also available are general and activity-specific blackline masters, for transparencies or for student worksheets, in the "Blackline Masters" section in The Diver Returns Unit Resources.

The Diver Returns Materials

- Poster of "As the Ferris Wheel Turns" blackline master
- (Optional) String and a small weight (such as a roll of tape)

More About Supplies

Graph paper is a standard supply for IMP classrooms. Blackline masters of 1-Centimeter Graph Paper, 1/4-Inch Graph Paper, and 1-inch Graph Paper are provided, for you to make copies and transparencies.

Assessing Progress

The Diver Returns concludes with two formal unit assessments. In addition, there are many opportunities for more informal, ongoing assessments throughout the unit. For more information about assessment and grading, including general information about the end-of-unit assessments and how to use them, consult *A Guide to IMP.*

End-of-Unit Assessments

This unit concludes with in-class and take-home assessments. The in-class assessment is intentionally short so that time pressures will not affect student performance. Students may use graphing calculators and their notes from previous work when they take the assessments. You can download unit assessments from the *The Diver Returns* Unit Resources.

Ongoing Assessment

One of the primary tasks of the classroom teacher is to assess student learning. Although the assigning of course grades may be part of this process, assessment more broadly includes the daily work of determining how well students understand key ideas and what level of achievement they have attained on key skills, in order to provide the best possible ongoing instructional program for them.

Students' written and oral work provides many opportunities for teachers to gather this information. We make some recommendations here of activities to monitor especially carefully that will give you insight into student progress.

- *As the Ferris Wheel Turns*
- *Free Fall*
- *The Simplified Dive, Revisited*
- *Big Push*
- *Complex Numbers and Quadratic Equations*
- *Three O'Clock Drop*
- *Vector Velocities*
- *The Diver's Success*

Discussion of Unit Assessments

Have students volunteer to explain their work on each of the problems. Encourage questions and alternate explanations from other students.

In-Class Assessment

In solving the equation in Question 1 by completing the square, students might first rewrite the equation as $x^2 + 4x = 3$ and then complete the square to get $(x + 2)^2 = 7$. The approximate solutions, to the nearest tenth, are 0.6 and −4.6.

For Question 2, students should sketch a parabolic graph going upward and with the two solutions from Question 1 as the x-intercepts. They might use the point
(0, −3) as a guide for the sketch.

For Question 3b, students should explain that the graph can have no x-intercepts (or cannot cross or touch the x-axis), since the equation has no "ordinary number" (real number) solutions.

Take-Home Assessment

The first step in solving the problem might be to find the components of Sabrina's initial velocity. Because the swing makes an angle of 30° with the vertical, Sabrina's initial path makes the same angle with the horizontal. Her overall speed is 30 feet per second, so the vertical component of her velocity is 30 · sin 30°, or exactly 15 feet per second (upward). That means her height after t seconds is
$11 + 15t - 16t^2$, so for Question 1, students need to solve the equation
$11 + 15t - 16t^2 = 1$. This gives a value for t of 1.4 seconds (to the nearest tenth).

For Question 2, students need to see that the horizontal component of Sabrina's speed is 30 · cos 30°, or approximately 26.0 feet per second. Using $t = 1.4$ means she travels about 36.4 feet in the horizontal direction. (If time and velocity are not rounded to tenths before multiplying, the value turns out to be closer to 36.1.)

For Question 3, Sabrina's vertical velocity after t seconds is $15 - 32t$. Using the rounded-off value of $t = 1.4$ gives this component when she hits the pad as 29.8 feet per second downward (although 29.4 feet per second is more accurate, as t is actually closer to 1.388 seconds). Her horizontal velocity is assumed to remain constant at 26.0 feet per second to the right. Finding her actual velocity, then, requires the Pythagorean theorem. Using the rounded-off values produces an actual velocity of 39.5 feet per second at impact (more exact values result in 39.2 feet per second).

Supplemental Activities

The unit contains a variety of activities at the end of the student pages that you can use to supplement the regular unit material. These activities fall roughly into two categories.

Reinforcements increase students' understanding and comfort with concepts, techniques, and methods that are discussed in class and are central to the unit.

Extensions allow students to explore ideas beyond those presented in the unit, including generalizations and abstractions of ideas.

The supplemental activities are presented in the teacher's guide and the student book in the approximate sequence in which you might use them. Below are specific recommendations about how each activity might work within the unit. You may wish to use some of these activities, especially the later ones, after the unit is completed.

Complex Conjugation **(extension)** This activity introduces the concept of the conjugate of a complex number and explores how this idea can be used to divide complex numbers, as well as the role of complex conjugates in the solution of quadratic equations. This activity can be used following the discussion of Complex Numbers and Quadratic Equations.

Absolutely Complex **(extension)** This activity introduces the concept of the absolute value of a complex number and asks students to explore its properties. It works well used together with the preceding supplemental activity, Complex Conjugation.

The Polar Complex **(extension)** This activity introduces the polar form of a complex number and how it can be used. It builds on ideas in the preceding supplemental activity, Absolutely Complex.

Polar Roots **(extension)** This activity extends the supplemental activity The Polar Complex to computation and verification of nth roots of complex numbers.

Number Research **(extension)** This activity is a natural follow-up to the introduction of imaginary numbers in Imagine a Solution and complex numbers in Complex Numbers and Quadratic Equations and Complex Components. It can be used anytime after those activities.

Back to the Circus

Intent

These activities introduce the central unit problem and review students' previous work with a simplified version of the problem in the Year 3 unit *High Dive.*

Mathematics

In *High Dive*, students solved the unit problem by making the simplifying assumption that the circular motion of the Ferris wheel does not affect the diver's falling motion. In these new activities, students briefly revisit the key steps in that development, including extending the sine and cosine functions to handle angles in all four quadrants and developing formulas relative to the motion of a freely falling object.

Progression

The new unit problem is introduced in the first activity. In most of the remaining activities, students review the solution of the simplified problem from *High Dive*.

First, students consider the motion of the diver while he is on the platform. The sine and cosine functions are redefined in a manner that makes them applicable to arbitrary angles, graphed, and used to develop expressions for the horizontal and vertical positions of the platform in *As the Ferris Wheel Turns* and *Graphing the Ferris Wheel.*

Students then look at the falling motion of the diver. *Distance with Changing Speed* develops a principle that allows students to easily find the average speed of an object undergoing constant acceleration, which enables the development of formulas for the analysis of a freely falling object in *Free Fall.*

The diver's movements before and after his release are combined to solve two simplified versions of the unit problem in *Moving Cart, Turning Ferris Wheel.* In *A Simple Summary and a Complex Beginning*, students summarize their work and begin to think about the complication presented by the effect of the Ferris wheel's circular motion on the falling diver.

The Circus Act
As the Ferris Wheel Turns
Graphing the Ferris Wheel
Distance with Changing Speed
Free Fall
Moving Cart, Turning Ferris Wheel
POW 1: Which Weights Weigh What?
Reference: The Standard POW Write-up
A Simple Summary and a Complex Beginning

The Circus Act

Intent

This activity introduces the central unit problem.

Mathematics

In the Year 3 unit *High Dive*, the central unit problem involved a circus act in which a diver was dropped from a turning Ferris wheel into a tub of water on a moving cart. Students were asked to determine how long after the Ferris wheel and cart began to move that the diver should be released. They were told to ignore the motion imparted to the diver by the movement of the Ferris wheel. In this new unit, students will return to that problem but without the simplification. They will now consider the effects of the Ferris wheel's turning on the falling motion of the diver.

Progression

Students sketch the path of the diver's motion for a release position in each quadrant of the Ferris wheel.

Approximate Time

45 minutes

Classroom Organization

Small groups, followed by whole-class discussion

Materials

Transparency of *The Circus Act* blackline master

Doing the Activity

Begin by explaining that this unit revisits the situation from the Year 3 unit *High Dive,* adding a new twist. You might have one or more students summarize what they recall of the situation or read the opening paragraphs of this activity aloud.

The cart and Ferris wheel are set up as shown below, with the cart passing in front of the Ferris wheel. The platform (not shown) points out from the page, perpendicular to the plane in which the Ferris wheel turns. The front end of the platform is directly above the path of the cart.

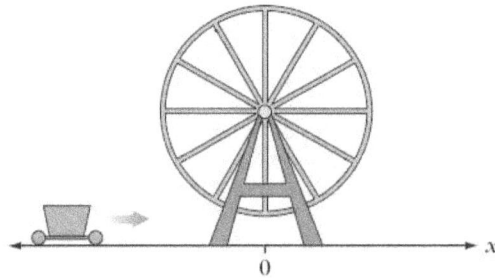

The intention of this activity is simply to get students intrigued about how the Ferris wheel's motion will affect the diver's path. You may find it helpful to have students imagine that the wheel is turning quite rapidly, so that the diver is "flung" from the wheel when he is released. They will not begin serious analysis of this change until *The Diver and the POW,* which begins to address the relevant physics principles about release from circular motion.

Discussing and Debriefing the Activity

Students will likely have a variety of ideas about the effect of the motion of the Ferris wheel on the path of the diver's fall. It's okay to leave the situation unresolved for now (though don't let students assume that any inaccurate ideas are correct). Eventually, they will see (or simply be told—see discussion of *A Simple Summary and a Complex Beginning*) that the diver's initial path is tangent to the circular path of his motion prior to release.

Focus the discussion on what happens for different release positions. For example, if the diver were released at the 12 o'clock position, he would be moving to the left at the moment of release. Ask, What would happen to the diver if he were released at the 12 o'clock position and there were no gravity? You may need to help students see that he would continue on a horizontal path.

Acknowledge that gravity *does* affect the diver's path, and ask how his landing position (after being released at the 12 o'clock position) would be different if he were released from a spinning rather than stationary Ferris wheel. How does the motion of the Ferris wheel affect the diver's landing position? Students will probably realize that he would end up farther to the left than if he were simply dropped straight down.

Have students do a similar analysis for release at some other time, such as the 4 o'clock position. What would happen at the 4 o'clock position without gravity? What about with gravity? Try to get agreement that in the absence of gravity, the diver would travel more or less upward to the right. Taking gravity into account, the diver's initial motion will cause him to end up farther to the right than if he were simply dropped. Students may also realize that it will take longer for him to reach the ground. The diagram illustrates what might happen if he were released at about the 4 o'clock position.

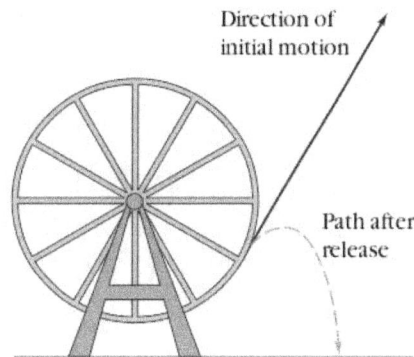

You might let students speculate as to how this complication will affect the final solution to the problem. Remind them that in the simplified version of the problem, the release takes place in the second quadrant.

Key Questions

What would happen to the diver if he were released at the 12 o'clock position and there were no gravity?

How does the motion of the Ferris wheel affect the diver's landing position?

What would happen at the 4 o'clock position without gravity? What about with gravity?

As the Ferris Wheel Turns

Intent

Students reexamine the relationship between time elapsed, clock position, and height on the Ferris wheel.

Mathematics

In this activity, students review the concept of angular velocity and the process of finding the height of the platform at any given time. The follow-up discussion reviews the extension of the sine and cosine functions to angles beyond those from right-triangle geometry.

Progression

Students work on the activity individually and discuss their results as a class.

Approximate Time

30 to 35 minutes for activity (at home or in class)
40 to 50 minutes for discussion

Classroom Organization

Individuals, followed by whole-class discussion

Materials

Poster of *As the Ferris Wheel Turns* blackline master for recording details of the Ferris wheel parameters

Doing the Activity

This activity requires little or no introduction.

Discussing and Debriefing the Activity

Questions 1 to 3

For Question 1, students will need to use the circumference formula, $C = 2\pi r$, to see that the total distance traveled by the platform in one complete turn is 100π feet. Because the platform goes 100π feet in 40 seconds, it is moving at

2.5π feet per second, or approximately 7.85 feet per second (roughly 5 miles per hour).

Post this result about the platform's speed, because it will be used later in the unit: **The speed of the platform as it turns is 2.5π feet per second, or approximately 7.85 feet per second.**

You may want to incorporate this information into a posted diagram of the Ferris wheel, marking each detail as it is discussed.

For Question 2, students should see that because a complete turn is 360°, the Ferris wheel must be turning 360 ÷ 40 = 9 degrees each second. Review the term *angular speed,* a measure of how fast an angle is changing, given in units such as degrees per second.

You may want to have a student identify the angle involved—namely, the angle between the radius to the platform and some fixed radius such as the one to the 3 o'clock position. Emphasize that angular speed involves a change in direction and does not depend on the Ferris wheel's radius.

For Question 3, students might find the angles first and then divide the number of degrees by 9, or they might express each turn as a fraction of a complete circle and then take that fraction of 40 seconds. For instance, in part a, the angle is 120°, or $\frac{1}{3}$ of a complete turn, so the time can be written as 120 ÷ 9 or as $\frac{1}{3}$ of 40.

Ask, **What word is used to describe the time interval for each complete turn of the Ferris wheel?** If necessary, remind students of the term *period*.

Question 4

Questions 4a and 4b are the easiest part of Question 4, as they involve angles in the first quadrant. Use the presentations of these problems to help students work out the details of getting from the time elapsed to the angle of turn, as well as the process of using trigonometry to get the platform's height from the angle of turn.

For example, for $t = 6$, the situation might be represented with the diagram shown here, in which y is the platform's height relative to the center of the wheel. The angle is 6 · 9° because the wheel turns 9 degrees per second. Students will probably use the equation $\sin 54° = \frac{y}{50}$ to get $y = 50 \sin 54°$. Therefore, the total height off the ground is $h = 65 + 50 \sin 54°$.

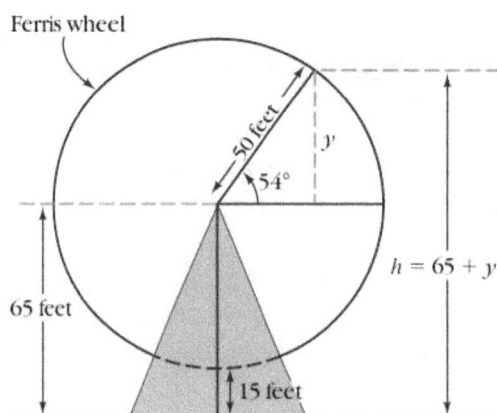

For Questions 4c and 4d, some students might simply use the expression 65 + 50 sin (9*t*). Others may go back to right-triangle trigonometry, using a right triangle within the second or third quadrant to analyze the situation. For Question 4c, some may simply recognize that *t* = 14 gives an angle that is the supplement of the case in Question 4a, so both problems yield the same height. The discussion should reflect all of these ideas, with students confirming that they get the same answer using all of these methods.

Use the discussion to review the principles for extending the sine function to all quadrants. As needed, go over the general definition, using a diagram like this:

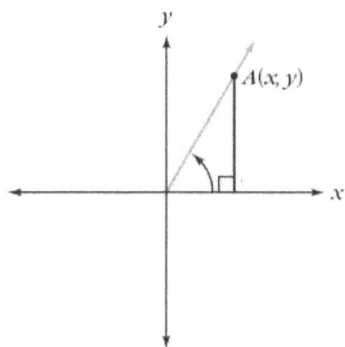

For a point *A* = (*x*, *y*) on the line and in the first quadrant, we have

$$\sin \theta = \frac{y}{\sqrt{x^2+y^2}}$$

We use that relationship for the general definition (or use points on the unit circle, so that the denominator is 1). Remind students of the convention of using r for the expression $\sqrt{x^2+y^2}$, which is the distance from A to the origin.

For points on the Ferris wheel, $\sqrt{x^2+y^2}$ is always 50, and the definition thus says that $y = 50 \sin \theta$. You might emphasize that $\sin \theta$ is negative in the third and fourth quadrants, reflecting the fact that the platform is below the center of the Ferris wheel, so the platform's height off the ground is $65 + 50 \sin \theta$.

Vertical Position on the Ferris Wheel

Remind students that in *High Dive,* the cart started moving as the platform passed the 3 o'clock position. You may want to post these two key results:
After t seconds, the platform has turned through an angle of 9t degrees.
After t seconds, the platform's height off the ground (in feet) is given by the expression 65 + 50 sin (9t).

Horizontal Position on the Ferris Wheel

Remind students that horizontal position is measured relative to the point directly below the center of the Ferris wheel, with the positive direction to the right. The cart starts to the left of the 0 point and moves to the right.

Ask students to find the platform's horizontal coordinate for each of the times from Question 4, and use the resulting discussion to review the extended definition of the cosine function. The diagram used for discussion of extending the sine function can be used to show the first-quadrant relationship $\cos \theta = \dfrac{x}{\sqrt{x^2+y^2}}$, which yields

$x = 50 \cos \theta$ for points on the Ferris wheel. This gives another key result:
After t seconds, the platform's horizontal position (in feet), relative to the center of the wheel, is given by the expression 50 cos (9t).

Ferris Wheel Parameters

At this point, review the full set of parameters for the circus act.
- The Ferris wheel has a radius of 50 feet.
- The center of the Ferris wheel is 65 feet off the ground.
- The Ferris wheel turns at a constant speed, making a complete turn every 40 seconds.
- The Ferris wheel turns counterclockwise.
- When the cart starts moving, it is 240 feet to the left of the center of the Ferris wheel's base.
- The cart travels to the right at a constant speed of 15 feet per second.
- The water level in the cart is 8 feet above the ground.
- When the cart starts moving, the diver's platform is at the 3 o'clock position.

Students should assume that when the cart starts moving, it is immediately traveling 15 feet per second. The final diagram of the situation might look like this (portions of this diagram are not to scale):

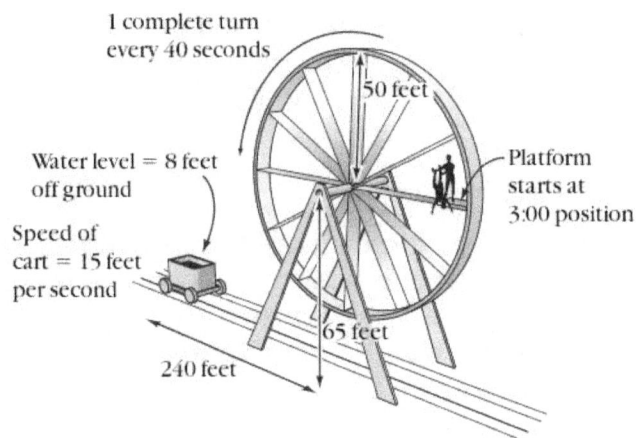

1 complete turn every 40 seconds

50 feet

Water level = 8 feet off ground

Platform starts at 3:00 position

Speed of cart = 15 feet per second

65 feet

240 feet

Key Question

What word is used to describe the time interval for each complete turn of the Ferris wheel?

Graphing the Ferris Wheel

Intent

Students graph the x- and y-coordinates of the platform as the Ferris wheel turns and consider how various parameters affect those graphs.

Mathematics

This activity reviews the graphs of the general sine and cosine functions, including variations in amplitude, period, and vertical displacement.

Progression

Students work on the activity individually. The subsequent discussion reviews the vocabulary of periodic functions.

Approximate Time

30 to 40 minutes for activity (at home or in class)
10 to 15 minutes for discussion

Classroom Organization

Individuals, followed by whole-class discussion

Doing the Activity

This activity requires little introduction.

Discussing and Debriefing the Activity

Question 1

Begin by asking about how students set up the graph for Question 1. How did you set up the axes and scales? The vertical scale should reflect the fact that the height goes from a minimum of 15 feet to a maximum of 115 feet.

Some students may have plotted individual points and then sketched a graph through them, while others may simply have recalled the general shape and used the given information to make appropriate adjustments. The graph should look something like this:

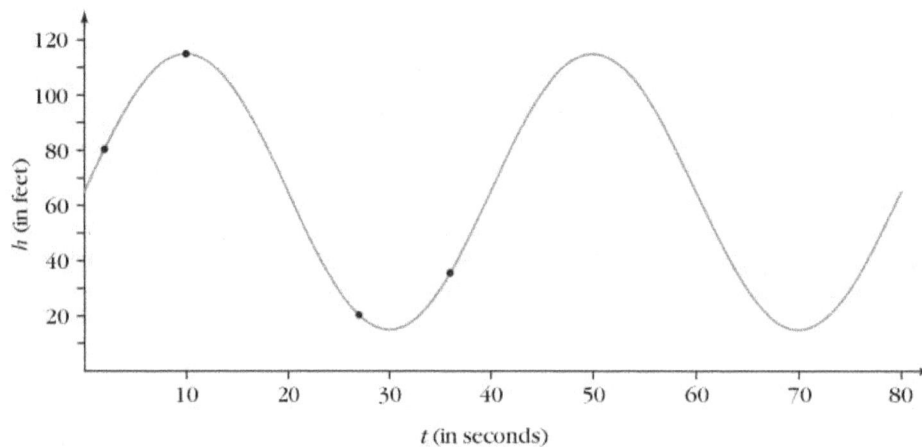

Ask **What single equation will describe the graph?** If needed, review the discussion from *As the Ferris Wheel Turns,* so students see that this is the graph of the equation $h = 65 + 50 \sin (9t)$.

Question 2

The discussion for Question 2 can be brief, but you might note that *x* here is the dependent variable, with *t* as the independent variable. The graph should look like this:

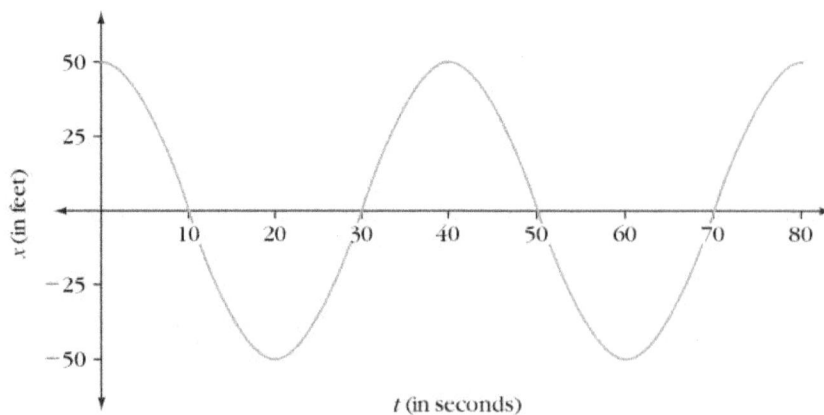

Question 3

The discussion of Question 3 can be limited to a qualitative description of the changes in the graphs.

For part a, students should be able to explain that if the radius were smaller, the graph from Question 1 would not go as "high" or as "low" as the original. They might describe the new graph as "squished vertically toward the line $y = 65$." Raise the idea that the "midline" of the graph remains the same. That is, the graph is still as much above the line $y = 65$ as it is below it.

Review that half the difference from high to low is called the *amplitude* of this graph. So, the amplitude for such a "Ferris wheel height graph" is the same as the Ferris wheel's radius. For the graph in Question 2, changing the radius also changes the amplitude.

For part b, students should see that if the wheel turns faster, the platform will go up and down more times during an 80-second interval. In other words, the height function will have a smaller period. They might describe the graph as "squished horizontally like an accordion." The graph from Question 2 will be affected in the same way.

Finally, for part c, students should see that the graph from Question 1 is just moved down so that it is above the axis half the time and below the axis half the time. Ask, **What has happened to the amplitude?** Students should see that the amplitude is unchanged. The graph from Question 2 is not affected by this change.

Key Questions

How did you set up the axes and scales?
What single equation will describe the graph?
What has happened to the amplitude?

Distance with Changing Speed

Intent

Students develop a method for finding the total distance traveled in situations involving constant acceleration.

Mathematics

In the introduction to this activity, students see that they can express total distance traveled in terms of the area under the graph of the speed function. This leads to a discovery that under constant acceleration, the average speed for a time interval is the average of the initial and final speeds for that interval.

Progression

After an introduction to using an area model to represent distance in terms of speed, students work on this activity individually. The follow-up discussion establishes the principle of averaging the initial and final speeds for an interval of constant acceleration in order to obtain the average speed.

Approximate Time

5 to 10 minutes for introduction
15 to 20 minutes for activity (at home or in class)
10 minutes for discussion

Classroom Organization

Individuals, followed by whole-class discussion

Materials

Transparency of *Distance with Changing Speed* blackline master

Doing the Activity

Remind students that one type of motion they will be considering is that of the falling diver, whose speed changes as he falls. Explain that because the speed is changing, the relationship among the variables of distance, speed, and time is more complex than if the speed were constant. To understand this complex situation, students will develop a simple model, using a graph, for representing the distance a moving object (or person) travels in terms of its speed.

Begin by posing this straightforward question: Suppose a person drives for
3 hours at a constant speed of 50 miles per hour. How far does the person
go?

All students need to do is multiply the speed (50 miles per hour) by the time
(3 hours) to get the distance (150 miles). Have them make a graph showing speed
as a function of time for this situation.

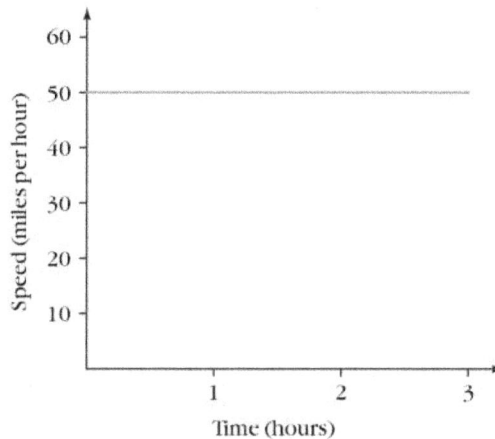

Then ask, How might you use this graph to represent the distance
geometrically? If needed, remind students that the area of a rectangle is often a
good model for multiplication. This should lead to a diagram like the one below.
Students should see that the area of this rectangle gives the value of the distance
traveled. You may want to suggest that they divide the rectangle as shown here to
indicate the distance covered each hour. (It may seem strange to use an area
model to represent a linear measurement. But because distance is the product of
rate and time, a two-dimensional model is appropriate.)

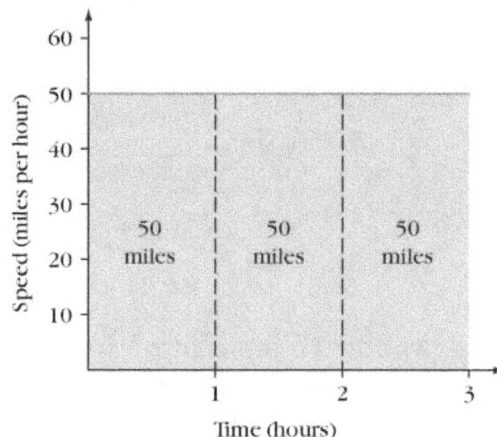

Discussing and Debriefing the Activity

Question 1 extends the use of the area model beyond the case of constant speed. For part a, students should get a diagram something like this one, showing speed as a function of time:

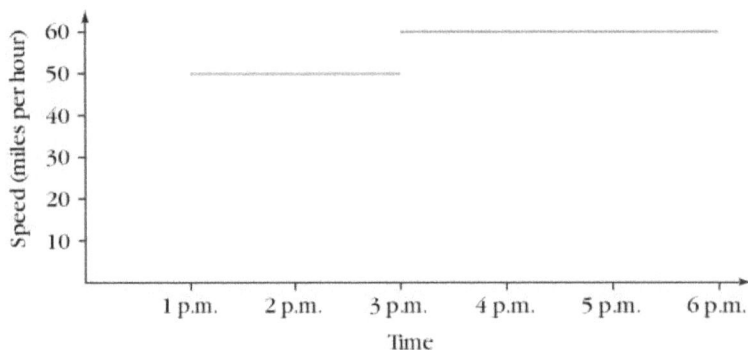

For part b, students might draw in the rectangles shown below to illustrate that the distance traveled from 1 p.m. to 3 p.m. is the area of the first rectangle and the distance traveled from 3 p.m. to 6 p.m. is the area of the second rectangle. Thus, the total area under the graph is equal to the total distance traveled.

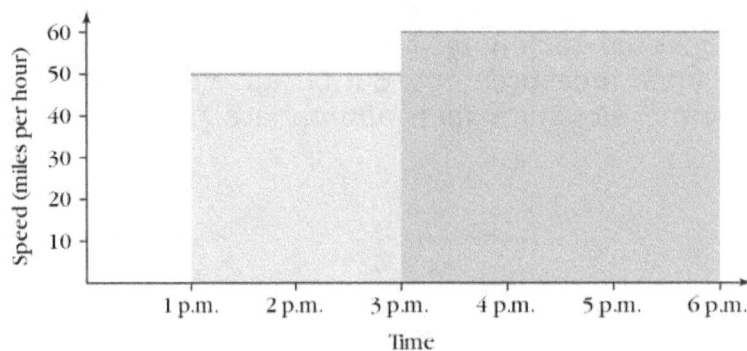

Question 2

Question 2 applies the new area model to a situation in which speed is changing at a constant rate. For part a, students should get a graph like the next one. You may want to use a transparency of this graph to aid in the discussion.

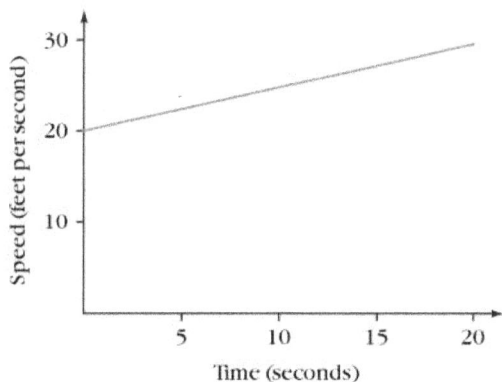

For part b, students will likely take an intuitive approach, saying that because the speed increases at a constant rate from 20 feet per second to 30 feet per second, the average speed is 25 feet per second. The goal is to confirm this intuitive approach by using the area model. Based on the earlier examples, students should accept that the total distance traveled ought to be equal to the area under the graph, as shown here:

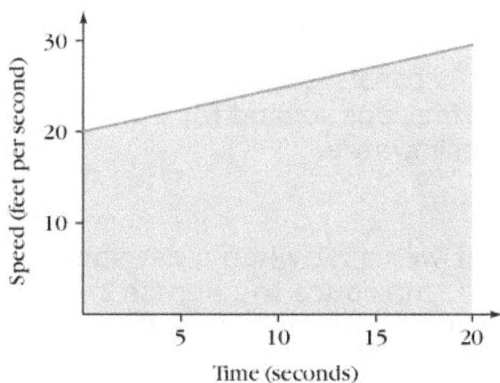

Ask, **How do you find the area of this shaded figure?** Students might note that the figure is a trapezoid, and they might even recall the formula for the area of a trapezoid.

To help suggest an intuitive approach, ask, **What rectangle would have the same area, using the same base?** Students should see that the rectangle in the next diagram has the same area as the trapezoid.

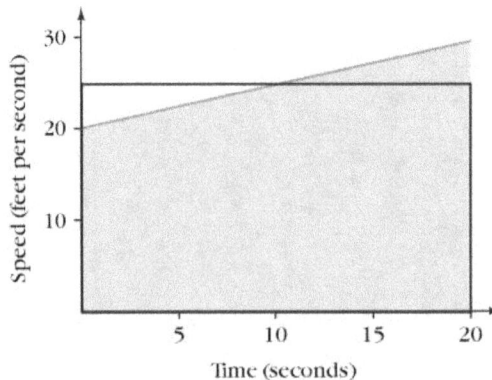

Students should also be able to see that the height of this rectangle is 25, which is the average of the heights of the two ends of the trapezoid, and that the area of the rectangle, and hence of the trapezoid, is 500. You may want to have them express the area in the form $\left(\frac{20+30}{2}\right) \cdot 20$ and review that this is an illustration of the general formula for the area of a trapezoid.

Ask, **What does the area mean in terms of the runner?** Help students see that it means the runner travels a total of 500 feet.

Finally, verify that this result is consistent with the intuitive answer to part b. That is, if the runner averaged 25 feet per second for 20 seconds, she would travel 500 feet, as found in part c using area.

What do we call the rate at which speed is changing? If no one comes up with the term, you might ask what we call it when a car speeds up. Students should think of the term *acceleration*. Introduce the phrase *constant acceleration* to describe the situation in Question 2, in which the speed is changing at a constant rate.

Averaging the Endpoints

Talk about the fact that the trapezoid approach will work for any situation involving constant acceleration and that it gives a simple way to find the total distance traveled, even though speed is not constant.

Ask students to sum up the principle for finding average speed in situations of constant acceleration. They should be able to articulate something like this, which you might post:

If an object is traveling with constant acceleration, its average speed

over any time interval is the average of its beginning and final speeds during that time interval.

We will refer to this principle as the "averaging the endpoints" method for finding average speed.

You might ask, How can this principle be used to find the total distance traveled? Students should see that, as always, they can multiply the average speed by the length of the time interval to get the total distance.

Key Questions

How might you use this graph to represent the distance geometrically?
How do you find the area of this shaded figure?
What rectangle would have the same area, using the same base?
What does the area mean in terms of the runner?
What do we call the rate at which speed is changing?

Free Fall

Intent

Students examine the behavior of falling objects.

Mathematics

In the introductory discussion, students recognize that falling objects accelerate and learn that this acceleration is constant. They then use the "averaging the endpoints" method to generalize equations for the distance an object falls in a given time and for the time required to fall a given distance.

Progression

The teacher introduces this activity with a brief discussion of falling objects. Students then work on the activity individually or in groups, before sharing findings in a class discussion.

Approximate Time

5 to 10 minutes for introduction
25 minutes for activity (at home or in class)
10 to 15 minutes for discussion

Classroom Organization

Individuals or small groups, followed by whole-class discussion

Doing the Activity

Begin by asking, What does the "averaging the endpoints" principle have to do with the main unit problem? If students don't see a connection, ask, What happens to an object as it falls freely?

If no one has a convincing argument that falling objects gain speed, you may want to bring up a situation like this for them to consider: Which would hurt more: a fall from your roof or a fall from your bed? Although this example relates more directly to the force of impact than to speed alone, most students will attribute the added force of falling from a roof to moving faster at impact.

Tell students that although experience tells us that objects go faster and faster as they fall, physicists actually know precisely how falling objects behave. From both experimental data and theoretical considerations, they know that falling objects have *constant acceleration.* You may want to post this statement, perhaps next to the description of the "averaging the endpoints" method:

> **Falling objects have constant acceleration (under ideal circumstances). That is, the speed of a falling object changes at a constant rate.**

Explain that "under ideal circumstances" means there is no wind, air resistance, or other complicating factor to interfere with the object's fall. That is, the principle describes the behavior of *free-falling objects.* You might mention that this assumption is not reasonable for some types of objects, such as feathers.

Discussing and Debriefing the Activity

Question 1

Question 1a should be straightforward. If students understood the introduction to the activity, they should see that the speed at $t = 5$ is simply $5 \cdot 32 = 160$ ft/s.

To find out how far an object falls in 5 seconds in Question 1b, students should reason that the object's average speed for that interval is equal to the average of its instantaneous speeds at the endpoints of the interval, $t = 0$ and $t = 5$. The instantaneous speed at $t = 0$ is 0 ft/s, the instantaneous speed at $t = 5$ is 160 ft/s, and the average of 0 and 160 is 80, so the object has an average speed over the 5-second interval of 80 ft/s. Therefore, the object falls $5 \cdot 80 = 400$ feet during this interval.

Question 2

The key element in this activity is for students to generalize the reasoning from Question 1 to develop the general expression in Question 2. They will likely see that the instantaneous speed at the end of t seconds is $32t$ and the instantaneous speed at the start is 0. Thus, the average speed over the first t seconds is $16t$ ft/s. They can then multiply this average speed by the length of the time interval, t seconds, to get a total distance traveled of $16t^2$ feet.

Post this conclusion, as it will play a critical role throughout the rest of the unit:

> **If an object falls freely from rest, it will fall $16t^2$ feet in the first t seconds.**

Questions 3 and 4

For Question 3, students simply need to subtract $16t^2$ from the initial height h to get the expression $h - 16t^2$ for the object's height after t seconds. Add this additional conclusion to the statement just posted:

> **If an object's initial height is h feet, its height after t seconds**

is **h − 16t² feet.**

Question 4 may seem straightforward once this expression has been found, but go over the transition carefully. For some students, it may be a substantial step from the idea of "reaching the ground" to the step of setting $h - 16t^2$ equal to 0. Help them to understand that answering Question 4 is equivalent to solving the equation $h - 16t^2 = 0$ for t in terms of h. Have a volunteer go through the details to get $t = \sqrt{\dfrac{h}{16}}$ seconds.

Post this additional generalization with the previous expression:

> **If an object falls freely from rest, it will take $\sqrt{\dfrac{h}{16}}$ seconds for it to fall h feet.**

Question 5

In Question 5, students need to see that the diver is actually falling 82 feet. They might set this up through the equation $90 - 16t^2 = 8$, or they might simply set $16t^2$ equal to 82. In either case, they should get the expression $\sqrt{\dfrac{82}{16}}$, which means it takes approximately 2.26 seconds for the diver to reach the water.

The Number 32 is an Approximation

At some point, mention that the number 32, which appears in *Free Fall*, is a numerical approximation based on experiments. Also point out that this number is specific to the use of feet as the unit of length. If we instead measure length in meters, for example, we use approximately 9.8 instead of 32 (as 32 feet is about 9.8 meters).

Key Questions

What does the "averaging the endpoints" principle have to do with the main unit problem?
What happens to an object as it falls freely?
Which would hurt more: a fall from your roof or a fall from your bed?

Moving Cart, Turning Ferris Wheel

Intent

Students solve the simplified version of the unit problem. Re-creating this simpler solution will prepare them to move on to a complete solution of the more complex problem.

Mathematics

Students will now solve the unit problem, but without taking into account the effects of the Ferris wheel's motion on the diver. The key to creating an equation for the unit problem is recognizing that the diver and the cart must be in the same place when the diver reaches water level. However, while setting the expressions from these two activities equal to each other creates an equation that completely describes the simplified unit problem, that equation defies solution by algebraic manipulation. It can be solved by an organized guess-and-check approach or, more elegantly, by using a calculator to approximate the intersection of the equations from the two earlier activities.

Progression

Students work through the development of the equation in small groups. (Though most students will have seen this activity in the previous year, encourage them to work their way through it again rather than trying to remember what they did before.) The class discussion focuses on the various methods used to solve the equation, including guess-and-check and graphing. This is also a good opportunity to review how to approach entry of complicated equations into the calculator (perhaps by breaking them into smaller pieces) and how to use the calculator's solve feature.

Approximate Time

65 minutes

Classroom Organization

Small groups, followed by whole-class discussion

Doing the Activity

Students need two more pieces of information before moving on to solve the simplified version of the problem. For the first, ask, Where will the cart be after t seconds? As needed, go over the fact that the cart starts 240 feet to the left of the Ferris wheel's base and travels to the right at 15 feet per second. This gives another key result:

After *t* seconds, the cart's horizontal position (in feet), relative to the center of the Ferris wheel, is given by −240 + 15*t*.

The second piece involves notation. The time variable *t* is used in this unit to represent the diver's time on the Ferris wheel before his release, the time of his fall, and the time of the cart's movement. To minimize confusion, in the Ferris wheel context we will sometimes use *W* for the time the diver spends on the wheel before his release and *F* for the time of his fall. The variable *W* is first introduced in this activity, and you might want to clarify its meaning. The variable *F* appears in *The Danger of Simplification*.

If students seem stuck, suggest they take a guess for *W* and see what happens to the diver and the cart if the diver is released after *W* seconds.

As students work, you might help them to focus on the idea that the cart and the diver must be in the same place when the diver reaches the water level. Ask, What two things have to be the same for the circus act to be successful? A key step is recognizing that if the diver is released after *W* seconds, he needs to fall 57 + 50 sin (9*W*) feet. Another is recognizing that the cart is moving while the diver is on the platform and while he is falling.

This rather formidable equation is one possibility that students may develop:

$$-240 + 15\left(W + \sqrt{\frac{57 + 50\ \sin\ (9W)}{16}}\right) = 50\ \cos\ (9W)$$

Once students get this or an equivalent equation, they might try to solve it algebraically and quickly find they are getting nowhere. The discussion below suggests several approaches for obtaining an estimate of the solution.

Discussing and Debriefing the Activity

Let several students present their analyses of the problem. Help them as needed to get an equation, such as this one noted previously:

$$-240 + 15\left(W + \sqrt{\frac{57 + 50\ \sin\ (9W)}{16}}\right) = 50\ \cos\ (9W)$$

Make sure students can articulate that the left side of the equation gives the *x*-coordinate of the cart at the time the diver is at water level, and the right side gives the *x*-coordinate of the diver at that same time. In other words, the equation is saying that the diver is landing in the water.

If students come up with variations on this equation, have them present their approaches and articulate the meaning of their equations.

Help students appreciate that this analysis is "quadrant-free." That is, it works no matter where the platform is when the diver is released.

Solving the Equation

Here are three ways students might solve the equation just developed:

- Guess-and-check: Pick a value for W, evaluate both sides, and repeatedly adjust W to bring the two sides of the equation closer together.
- Graphing: For instance, graph the two functions defined by the expressions on the two sides of the equation and then look at where the graphs meet. This will require adjusting the window settings to locate the point of intersection.
- Using the calculator's solve feature.

It turns out that the assistant should release the diver about 12.28 seconds after the cart starts moving. If students haven't already done so, have them substitute $W = 12.28$ into the equation to confirm this result.

Using the Result

Be sure to address the question of where the platform is on the Ferris wheel when the diver is released. After 12.28 seconds, the Ferris wheel will have turned $9 \cdot 12.28 \approx 110.5°$, placing the platform between the 11 o'clock and 12 o'clock positions.

The diver's height off the ground when he is released is given by the expression $65 + 50 \sin (9W)$, for a value of about 112 feet. The diver's x-coordinate is given by $50 \cos (9W)$, which comes out to about −17.5, meaning he is about 17.5 feet to the left of center.

Students will probably want to work out more of the stages in the process for $W = 12.28$. For example, the diver must fall about $112 − 8 = 104$ feet, which will take about $\sqrt{\dfrac{104}{16}} \approx 2.55$ seconds. Thus, the cart must travel a total of about $12.28 + 2.55 = 14.83$ seconds. Multiplying by 15 feet per second and adding to −240 gives −17.55, almost perfectly matching the position of the diver.

Students have now recapitulated their work from the Year 3 unit *High Dive*. Part I of *A Simple Summary and a Complex Beginning* asks them to summarize their work so far, and in the discussion of that activity they will be asked to speculate on how their analysis will need to change for the more complex problem.

Key Questions

Where will the cart be after t seconds?
What two things have to be the same for the circus act to be successful?

POW 1: Which Weights Weigh What?

Intent

Students solve a difficult logic problem and communicate their reasoning in writing.

Mathematics

This POW involves looking for a pattern in a problem situation. Students are asked to find a procedure for choosing weights to be used on a balance scale that will allow the user to verify the largest number of sequential integer weights, beginning with 1. They are to do this both for a method in which the weights must all go on the opposite side of the scale from the item to be weighed and for a method in which some weights may be placed on the same side of the scale as the item. The problem can be extended by having students develop a proof for the sum of powers of 2 or by relating the first method to base 2 numeration.

Progression

Give students about a week to work on this POW. Part II of *The Diver and the POW* will help them get started. Presentations will follow.

Approximate Time

10 to 15 minutes for introduction
3 to 4 hours for activity (at home)
30 to 35 minutes for presentations and discussion

Classroom Organization

Individuals, followed by whole-class presentations and discussion

Doing the Activity

You might have volunteers read the POW aloud. You may want to clarify what the task is, emphasizing that students are to consider each method separately.

Part II of *The Diver and the POW* will help students get started on the problem for a review of how to write up their results. Refer them to *Reference: The Standard POW Write-up*.

On the day before the POW is due, select several students to make presentations of their solutions the following day.

Discussing and Debriefing the Activity

Discuss each method separately, beginning with presentations on the first (and simpler) method, letting other students contribute, and then moving to the second method.

Method 1: Combining Weights on One Side

If the presentations on this method do not examine specific examples in detail, discuss at least a couple of cases, such as two weights and then three weights.

For all cases, the first weight must be a 1 ounce, because otherwise it's impossible to verify the weight of a 1-ounce package. For two weights, the second weight must be 2 ounces (the only other option is another 1-ounce weight, which is less useful); the king can then verify the weights of packages up to 3 ounces.

Similarly, for three weights, the first two weights must be 1 and 2 ounces, so the third should be 4 ounces (the least amount that can't be verified with the first two). The king can then verify the weights of packages up to 7 ounces.

Help students see that they can proceed systematically, at each stage adding a new weight that is 1 ounce more than the sum of the previous weights. At each stage, no matter what weights the king has, the largest weight he can verify is the sum of his weights.

Students will probably realize that the desired weights are all powers of 2 (starting with 2^0, which equals 1) and that with these n weights, the king can verify the weights of packages up to $2^n - 1$ ounces.

Optional: Powers of 2 and the Base 2 Numeration System

This problem offers the opportunity for some interesting digressions. Here are two ideas you might pursue:
- Have students prove that the sum of the first n powers of 2 (starting with 2^0) is $2^n - 1$.
- Use the idea of sums of powers of 2 to introduce the base 2 numeration system. The general principle for Method 1 is essentially the same as the idea that every positive integer can be expressed using 0s and 1s in this numeration system.

Method 2: Using Weights on Both Sides

Method 2 is more complex, as it essentially involves both sums and differences.

For the case of two weights, students should see that if the king's weights are 1 ounce and 2 ounces, he can verify packages of 1, 2, or 3 ounces, but if his weights are 1 and 3, he can verify packages of 1, 2, 3, or 4 ounces.

Some students may think that using weights of 2 and 3 ounces might be even better, because it is still possible to verify the weight of a 1-ounce package and this combination allows the king to verify the weight of a 5-ounce package. But this pair doesn't allow for weighing a 4-ounce package. You might ask students to try to prove in detail that no pair of weights is better than 1 and 3.

In general, with n weights, the optimal selection is to have weights that are the first n powers of 3, starting from 3^0. For instance, if the king is selecting four weights, he should choose 3^0, 3^1, 3^2, and 3^3 ounces.

Whatever the weights are, the largest weight the king can verify is the sum of his weights. If the weights are 1, 3, 9, . . . , 3^{n-1}, the sum turns out to be $\frac{3^n - 1}{2}$. For example, when n is 4, the weights 1, 3, 9, and 27 can be used to verify the weight of any package from 1 through $\frac{3^4 - 1}{2}$; that is, from 1 through 40 ounces.

Reference: The Standard POW Write-up

Intent

Students are given the format and content expectations for completing their Problem of the Week write-ups throughout the course.

Mathematics

While the mathematical content will vary with each POW, the exercise of writing up the results will play an important role in reinforcing that content. In most cases, the benefits of carefully completing the write-up will arguably be greater than those of mastering the mathematics. The ability to order their thoughts and to present them in a clear, precise manner will deepen and solidify students' understanding of the relevant mathematical principles in a given POW.

Progression

Students who used the IMP Year 3 curriculum will be familiar with what is expected in POW write-ups. This material is presented primarily as reference for their use.

Approximate Time

10 minutes (at home)

Classroom Organization

Individual reference

Doing the Activity

Suggest that students read *Reference: The Standard POW Write-up* before beginning their first POW write-up.

You may want to take the time to present your general expectations for POWs and review the categories. In particular, you might discuss what role, if any, the self-grading students do in the self-assessment category will play in the grades you assign.

A Simple Summary and a Complex Beginning

Intent

Students summarize their progress on the unit problem, reflecting upon the formulas they have developed, and begin to consider the effects of the Ferris wheel's motion on the diver.

Mathematics

Students compile the formulas they have used so far and speculate on how they will need to adjust them for the more complex version of the problem. They then look at a gravity-free analogy to the diver's release to help them understand how the circular motion of the Ferris wheel platform affects the diver's motion.

Progression

An optional demonstration will help students get a feel for how the Ferris wheel's motion affects the path of the diver. Students work on the two parts of the activity individually and share findings in a class discussion.

Approximate Time

10 minutes for introduction
30 minutes for activity (at home or in class)
20 minutes for discussion

Classroom Organization

Individuals, followed by whole-class discussion

Materials

Transparency of the *A Simple Summary and a Complex Beginning* blackline master
Optional: String and a small weight (such as a roll of tape) for demonstrating a release from circular motion

Doing the Activity

You may want to introduce the activity with this optional demonstration. For safety reasons, it might be best to conduct it outdoors. Test this demonstration before doing it for the class.

Tie an object, such as a roll of masking tape or a chalkboard eraser, to the end of a piece of string about 4 feet long. The object should be heavy enough to create minimal air resistance, but soft enough to prevent serious injury. Spin around, swinging the object around yourself in a circle at a more or less constant height. Then let go of the string and watch the object fly.

Help students notice two things about the object's path of flight:
- The object continues in a straight line (except that it sinks to the ground). It does not continue in its original circular path, although people's intuition often suggests that it should.
- That straight line is tangent to the circle. For example, if you are turning counterclockwise and facing north when you let go, the object will fly west.

If you allow students to experiment, keep in mind that they may not have good control over timing the release of the string.

Discussing and Debriefing the Activity

Part I: A Simple Summary

Make a class list of the formulas students used to solve the problem. The key formulas are these, based on releasing the diver after W seconds:
- Diver's height at time of release: $65 + 50 \sin (9W)$
- Diver's horizontal coordinate at time of release: $50 \cos (9W)$
- Distance the diver falls: $57 + 50 \sin (9W)$
- Time the diver falls: $\sqrt{\dfrac{57 + 50 \sin (9W)}{16}}$

- Time the cart travels until the diver reaches the water level:
$$W + \sqrt{\frac{57 + 50 \sin (9W)}{16}}$$
- Cart's horizontal coordinate when diver reaches the water level:
$$-240 + 15\left(W + \sqrt{\frac{57 + 50 \sin (9W)}{16}}\right)$$

Students may express these formulas in different ways, combine them, or break them down further. Save the list so that students can refer to it in *An Expanded Portfolio of Formulas*.

For Question 2, make sure someone points out that the cart's horizontal coordinate must be the same as that of the diver for the circus act to be a success.

Ask, How might these formulas need to change for the more complex version of the problem? Bring out that the first three expressions listed above will be unchanged, because they relate only to what happens before the diver is released. But at this point, it is probably unclear to students whether the time for his fall will change, and this could affect the time that the cart travels until the diver reaches water level, which in turn would change the cart's position when the diver reaches the water.

One other change you might mention is that although the diver's horizontal coordinate at the time of release will still be 50 cos (9W), this horizontal positioning may change as he falls, requiring a new expression.

Part II: A Complex Beginning

Let students share ideas about Question 3. Many may think that the skateboarder will continue in a circular, or at least curving, path, as shown here.

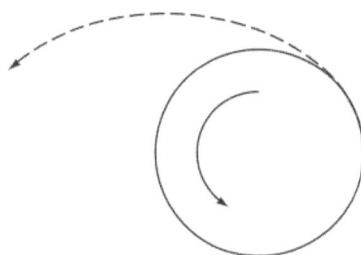

In fact, a person traveling in a circular path and then released would travel in a direction tangent to the circular path, as shown below. (You may want to project this diagram.)

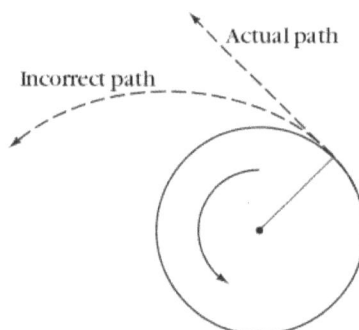

Help students understand that the tangent to a circle is perpendicular to the circle's radius at the point of tangency. This fact will be useful in determining certain angles involved in the diver's initial motion as he leaves the Ferris wheel. Post the principle for students' reference:

> **In the absence of external forces such as gravity, an object released from a circular path will travel in a straight line. That straight-line path forms a right angle with the circle's radius to the point of release.**

In Part I of *The Diver and the POW,* students will need to consider the implications of the principle just stated. Because of the role of gravity, the Ferris wheel situation is more complex, and in fact, the diver does actually move along a curved path (unless he is initially traveling either straight up or straight down).

Ask, **How fast would an object be going when first released?** Students may have various ideas on this, and you may have to simply tell them this principle:

> **When an object is released from a circular path, it will have an initial speed equal to the speed at which it was already traveling.**

Key Questions

How might these formulas need to change for the more complex version of the problem?
How fast would an object be going when first released?

A Falling Start

Intent

In these activities, students examine the effects of an initial vertical speed on a falling body.

Mathematics

Students now begin to look at the effect of the turning of the Ferris wheel on the diver's fall. They examine the simplest cases, those in which the initial motion is purely vertical. Along the way, they consider the use of the quadratic formula for solving the quadratic equations that arise in situations involving falling objects. This leads to a short digression concerning imaginary and complex numbers.

Progression

In *The Diver and the POW,* students consider, in a general way, the complexity of the combined effects of the vertical and horizontal motion imparted to the diver by the Ferris wheel.

A more exact analysis of situations involving only initial vertical motion begins with *Look Out Below!* and *Big Push,* where the initial motion is downward. The quadratic expressions that emerge motivate the introduction of the quadratic formula in *Finding with the Formula.* Students look at some of the difficulties that arise in applying the formula in *Using Your ABCs.* One of those difficulties—that of a negative radicand—leads to the introduction of imaginary and then complex numbers in *Imagine a Solution, Complex Numbers and Quadratic Equations,* and *Complex Components,* which also introduces vectors.

Three O'Clock Drop and *Up, Down, Splat!* turn the focus back to falling bodies having initial vertical motion, this time when that initial motion is upward.

Finally, *Falling Time for Vertical Motion* asks students to generalize their work so far by using the quadratic formula to develop an expression for the falling time of a freely falling body with initial vertical motion.

Look Out Below!
The Diver and the POW
Big Push
Finding with the Formula
Using Your ABCs
Imagine a Solution
Complex Numbers and Quadratic Equations
Complex Components

Three O'Clock Drop
Up, Down, Splat!
Falling Time for Vertical Motion

Look Out Below!

Intent

Students examine a situation involving an object falling with initial downward speed.

Mathematics

In *Free Fall,* students developed formulas to assist in the analysis of the motion of an object falling freely from rest. The diver in the unit problem, however, has an initial speed imparted by the turning Ferris wheel. Now students consider how to modify one of their equations to allow for an initial downward speed.

In this activity, they develop an expression for the height of a pillow falling downward as a function of time using the "averaging the endpoints" method of finding average speed. Solving for the time the pillow takes to reach the ground leads to a quadratic equation, which is used to review the method of completing the square.

Progression

The class reviews the concept of constant acceleration and the "averaging the endpoints" method before students work in groups on the activity. The follow-up discussion includes a review of the "completing the square" technique and a lead-in to a more substantial discussion of quadratic equations in conjunction with *Finding with the Formula*.

Approximate Time

55 to 65 minutes

Classroom Organization

Small groups, preceded and followed by whole-class discussion

Doing the Activity

Before groups begin, review the idea of constant acceleration and the method of "averaging the endpoints" by revisiting Question 1 of *Free Fall.* For instance, ask, If an object falls freely from rest, what is its instantaneous speed after 5 seconds? What is its average speed for those 5 seconds? How far does it fall in that time?

Review the principle that this object's average speed is the average of its initial speed (0, because the object is falling from rest) and its final speed (32 · 5 feet per second). Emphasize that this principle holds because acceleration is constant. Once students have the average speed, they can get the distance traveled by multiplying average speed by time spent traveling.

Point out that although this new activity involves another falling object, the rate of acceleration here is different, because air resistance has a significant effect on the pillow's motion. (In fact, as noted in the activity, air resistance will cause the pillow to accelerate at a nonconstant rate.)

You may want to work through Question 1 as a class to be sure the situation is clear.

If students need assistance with Question 4, have them suppose that the fall took t seconds. They should then find expressions for the pillow's instantaneous speed t seconds after Maxine sees it, for its average speed for the first t seconds, and for the distance it travels in those t seconds. This should lead to a quadratic expression for the distance the pillow falls in t seconds. Students can use a guess-and-check or graphing approach to solve the related equation.

Discussing and Debriefing the Activity

For Question 1, students should see that after 1 second, the pillow must be traveling 50 ft/s and, after 2 seconds, 70 ft/s.

For Question 2, the intent is for students to use the "averaging the endpoints" method. Thus, they should average the beginning speed (30 ft/s) with the instantaneous speed after 2 seconds (70 ft/s) to get an average speed of 50 ft/s for the interval from 0 to 2 seconds.

For Question 3, get an explicit statement of how to obtain the distance from this average speed, as this is a key step in the generalization required for Question 4. Students need to see that they must multiply the average speed (50 ft/s) by the time interval (2 seconds) to find that the pillow falls 100 feet during the 2 seconds.

For Question 4, using t for the time the fall took, students will likely begin the explanation by noting that the instantaneous speed after t seconds is $30 + 20t$ ft/s, so the average speed for the first t seconds is $\frac{30 + (30 + 20t)}{2}$ ft/s. You might ask a volunteer to simplify this expression and then have the class verify that the simplified expression, $30 + 10t$, gives the value 50 when $t = 2$, consistent with the answer to Question 2.

The next step is to multiply this average speed by the length of the time interval, which gives the expression $t(30 + 10t)$, or $30t + 10t^2$, as the distance traveled in t seconds. Again, you might have students check that for $t = 2$, this matches their earlier result. They will probably then simply set this expression equal to 200 feet (the distance the pillow needs to fall) to get the equation $30t + 10t^2 = 200$.

Once this equation is found, ask, **What type of equation is this? What is its standard form?** Have the class identify this as a quadratic equation and put it into standard quadratic form, perhaps simplifying it to

$$t^2 + 3t - 20 = 0$$

Solving by Completing the Square

Although students may have solved the equation using a guess-and-check approach (getting 3.2 seconds, to the nearest tenth), have them look at the solution algebraically as well.

As needed, review the technique of completing the square. Students might begin by writing the equation as $t^2 + 3t = 20$ and then look for a constant term to add to both sides so that the left side becomes a perfect square. You might review the use of a diagram like this one for this process:

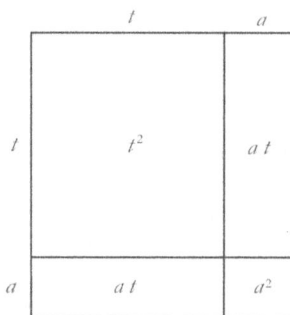

Because we want a square, the two sides are the same. The two rectangles with area at combine to give $3t$, so $a = 1.5$, and the small section has an area of 2.25. Adding 2.25 to both sides gives $(t + 1.5)^2 = 22.25$, so $t + 1.5 = \pm\sqrt{22.25}$, or approximately ± 4.7. Since we are looking for the number of seconds, only a positive solution to this equation is needed. Thus, $t \approx 3.2$.

Question 5

Students should see that the pillow's height t seconds after Maxine sees it is given by the equation

$$h = 200 - 30t - 10t^2$$

Post this for comparison with similar equations in the discussion following *Big Push*.

One goal of Question 5 is for students to see the role played by the initial height, the initial speed, and the gravitational acceleration in determining the height of a falling object. To bring this out, ask, *Where do the coefficients in the expression 200 − 30t − 10t^2 come from?* Students should be able to identify 200 as the pillow's initial height and 30 as its initial speed.

It may be more difficult for students to state where the coefficient 10 comes from. Have them retrace their steps to see that it is half of 20, which is the rate of acceleration. (In the discussion of *Using Your ABCs,* students will develop a general equation for a falling object's height after *t* seconds.)

As noted previously, the pillow will meet substantial air resistance. This resistance increases as the pillow goes faster, so the rate of acceleration will not be constant. You may want to point out that the mathematical model described in the problem is actually not a good one for this situation.

Another Approach

Another method for solving this problem involves visualizing the pillow as having been dropped from rest from some higher altitude. One can determine, based on the acceleration rate, that the pillow has been falling for 1.5 seconds when Maxine sees it. During that time, it averages 15 feet per second (halfway between 0 and 30), so it has already traveled 22.5 feet. Thus, its initial height was 222.5 feet (adding in the 200 feet it drops after Maxine sees it). So *t* seconds after Maxine sees the pillow, it has been traveling *t* + 1.5 seconds, falling from rest from a height of 222.5 feet. The total fall takes $\sqrt{\dfrac{222.5}{10}}$ seconds (replacing 16 in the usual expression by 10), and the part of the fall after Maxine sees the pillow takes 1.5 seconds less.

Key Questions

If an object falls freely from rest, what is its instantaneous speed after 5 seconds? What is its average speed for those 5 seconds? How far does it fall in that time?
What type of equation is this? What is its standard form?
Where do the coefficients in the expression 200 − 30t − 10t^2 come from?

The Diver and the POW

Intent

Students consider the general effects on the diver of being released from the Ferris wheel at several clock positions.

Mathematics

In Part I, students apply ideas about release from circular motion to the Ferris wheel situation, from an intuitive perspective. In Part II, they consider a problem similar to the situation in the POW to help them develop ideas for the POW.

Progression

Students work on the activity individually and share ideas in a class discussion.

Approximate Time

25 minutes for activity (at home or in class)
15 minutes for discussion

Classroom Organization

Individuals, followed by whole-class discussion

Doing the Activity

This activity requires little or no introduction.

Discussing and Debriefing the Activity

Part I

For Question 1, bring out that if the diver is moving partly upward at the moment of release, his falling time will be increased by the effect of the motion of the Ferris wheel's motion. If he is moving partly downward when released, his falling time will be decreased by the effect of the Ferris wheel's motion. Students might answer the question using a description like this or, more specifically, in terms of Ferris wheel positions. For instance, they might say that the diver's falling time is increased if he is on the right side of the wheel (moving upward from the 6 o'clock to the 12 o'clock position, counterclockwise).

Similarly, for Question 2, students should see that if the diver is moving to the left (right) when he is released, he will land to the left (right) of his release position.

There is no purely intuitive way to answer Question 3. With the diver being released between the 12 o'clock and 11 o'clock positions, here are the issues:

- The wheel's motion will cause the diver to reach the water sooner. This means the cart will not have traveled as far when the diver reaches the water. This effect, taken by itself, suggests that the assistant should hold onto the diver longer to allow the cart more time to travel.
- The wheel's motion will cause the diver to be farther to the left when he reaches the water, which means the cart doesn't have to go as far. This effect, taken by itself, suggests that the assistant should hold onto the diver for less time.

You may want to let students discuss this in their groups for a few minutes and then share their ideas. There is no simple way to see how to balance these two effects. Tell students they will have to work out the numerical details of the situation to answer the question. (Students will actually answer this question in *The Danger of Simplification.*)

Part II

You can begin by having a student answer the specific questions in the problem. Students should see that to get 10 ounces, they can begin by filling an 8-ounce cup and pouring from it to fill the 6-ounce cup. This leaves 2 ounces in the 8-ounce cup. They can use these 2 ounces and add a full 8-ounce measure to get 10 ounces. More generally, they should see also that variations on this procedure allow them to get any multiple of 2 ounces. On the other hand, they should see that they cannot measure amounts that are an odd number of ounces.

Ask for volunteers to discuss the similarities and differences between this problem and the situation in the POW. They should see, for example, that just as filling the 6-ounce cup from the 8-ounce cup leaves 2 ounces in the 8-ounce cup, so also putting an 8-ounce weight on one side of the scale and a 6-ounce weight on the other will allow the king to verify the weight of a 2-ounce object.

On the other hand, they should see that in the POW, if the king has just two weights, of 6 ounces and 8 ounces, then he cannot confirm the weight of anything above 14 ounces.

Big Push

Intent

Students calculate how the diver's falling time would be affected if he were released from the Ferris wheel with a purely downward initial speed.

Mathematics

This problem is basically a Ferris wheel version of *Look Out Below!* Students calculate the falling time for the diver to reach the water level from the 9 o'clock position of both a moving and a stationary Ferris wheel. They compare the answers to see how far the diver would miss by if he neglected to take into account the initial speed imparted by the wheel's motion. Finding the falling time involves solving a quadratic equation.

Progression

Students work on the activity individually or in groups. The follow-up discussion briefly reviews the technique of solving an equation by completing the square.

Approximate Time

25 to 30 minutes for activity (at home or in class)
10 minutes for discussion

Classroom Organization

Individuals or small groups, followed by whole-class discussion

Doing the Activity

This activity requires little or no introduction.

Discussing and Debriefing the Activity

The analysis is essentially the same as that for *Look Out Below!,* except for these details:

- The initial height is 65 feet instead of 200 feet.
- The diver needs to reach a height of only 8 feet rather than reach the ground.
- The initial speed is 7.85 ft/s (2.5π ft/s) instead of 30 ft/s.
- The acceleration is 32 ft/s per second instead of 20 ft/s.

For Question 1, students should find that the height after t seconds is given by the equation

$$h = 65 - 7.85t - 16t^2$$

Save this equation for comparison with the equations from *Look Out Below!* and from Question 2c of *Using Your ABCs* in the discussion that introduces *Three O'Clock Drop.*

For Question 2, students need to take into account that the water level is 8 feet off the ground. They should come up with an equation equivalent to $65 - 7.85t - 16t^2 = 8$ and find (probably by guess-and-check) that it takes approximately 1.66 seconds for the diver to reach the water.

In Question 3, students should see that if the diver is dropped from the 9 o'clock position of a stationary wheel, it will take $\sqrt{\dfrac{57}{16}} \approx 1.89$ seconds for him to reach the water. Therefore, the initial motion from the turning wheel shortens the time by about 0.23 second.

Question 4 asks the question, How far would the cart move in this amount of time? At 15 ft/s, it would travel about $0.23 \cdot 15 \approx 3.5$ feet (or 3.4 feet if students do not round at intermediate steps), so failure to take the diver's initial speed into account might cost him his life!

Key Question

How far would the cart move in this amount of time?

Finding with the Formula

Intent

This activity introduces the quadratic formula.

Mathematics

As students have seen in several recent activities, the height function for a falling object will always involve a quadratic equation. The class reviewed the technique of solving these equations by completing the square with the equation from *Look Out Below!* The introductory discussion of this new activity develops the quadratic formula using the technique of completing the square. The activity provides two practice problems to be solved with the quadratic formula, one of which has a negative value for the coefficient *b* and one of which is not presented in standard form.

Progression

The teacher introduces this activity with a quick look at how quadratic equations are related to the unit problem and then assists the class in developing the quadratic formula by solving the general quadratic equation. Students then work on the activity individually.

Approximate Time

15 to 20 minutes for introduction
15 to 20 minutes for activity (at home or in class)
10 minutes for discussion

Classroom Organization

Individuals, preceded and followed by whole-class discussion

Doing the Activity

Introduce the activity by pointing out that *Look Out Below!* and *Big Push* each involved finding the solutions to a quadratic equation. Get students to state those two equations, and display them for today's discussion. It isn't essential that the equations be in standard form. For example, they might look like this:

$$10t^2 + 30t = 200$$
$$65 - 7.85t - 16t^2 = 8$$

Ask, **Why do problems of this type lead to quadratic equations?** Students will probably recognize that average speed is a linear function of t, so multiplying the average speed by the time interval will give a quadratic expression.

Bring out that the coefficient 7.85 comes from a particular release position and that, in general, this coefficient will depend on when the diver is released. That means that to create a general equation for the falling time, students will have to solve an equation like the one from *Big Push,* but with an expression involving W in place of the specific value 7.85. Tell them that their next task will be to find a way to write the solution to any quadratic equation as an expression in terms of its coefficients.

Sketching a Solution by Completing the Square

Before students undertake that formidable task, remind them that they previously solved the equation $200 - 30t - 10t^2 = 0$ by simplifying and completing the square. Although the numbers in the equation from *Big Push* are messier than those from *Look Out Below!,* it's worthwhile to ask students to outline how they would solve $65 - 7.85t - 16t^2 = 8$ by that method.

For instance, they might begin by rewriting the equation as $16t^2 + 7.85t = 57$. Without having them do the arithmetic, have the class put into words what the remaining steps might be. You might have them redo the solution to $200 - 30t - 10t^2 = 0$ as a model.

Have students make the steps fairly explicit and write them down. They might come up with an outline like this:

1. Divide both sides by 16.
2. Take half the coefficient of t and think of that as the constant part of the squared term.
3. Add the square of that "half-coefficient" to both sides.
4. Write the left side as a perfect square.
5. Take the square root of both sides.
6. Subtract to get the value of t.

Try to get students to agree that this process would work even though the computations might be pretty messy.

The General Quadratic Equation

Ask, **What might the general quadratic equation look like?** If needed, review that the standard form is $ax^2 + bx + c = 0$.

Then ask students to apply their outline to this equation, doing the work in terms of the coefficients. (This may actually be easier than working with numbers.) Although you may need to help with the details, urge students to rely as much as possible on their outline. They might get this sequence of steps. (The issue of the two square roots is avoided in this sequence, but is addressed next.)

Subtract c from both sides to prepare for using the outline.	$ax^2 + bx = -c$
Step 1: Divide both sides by a.	$x^2 + \dfrac{b}{a}x = -\dfrac{c}{a}$
Step 2: Identify the "half-coefficient" as $\dfrac{b}{2a}$.	
Step 3: Add the square of the half-coefficient to both sides.	$x^2 + \dfrac{b}{a}x + \left(\dfrac{b}{2a}\right)^2 = -\dfrac{c}{a} + \left(\dfrac{b}{2a}\right)^2$
Step 4: Write the left side as a perfect square.	$\left(x + \dfrac{b}{2a}\right)^2 = -\dfrac{c}{a} + \left(\dfrac{b}{2a}\right)^2$
Step 5: Take the square root of both sides.	$x + \dfrac{b}{2a} = \sqrt{-\dfrac{c}{a} + \left(\dfrac{b}{2a}\right)^2}$
Step 6: Subtract to get the value of x.	$x = \sqrt{-\dfrac{c}{a} + \left(\dfrac{b}{2a}\right)^2} - \dfrac{b}{2a}$

The last step shows an unsimplified version of the quadratic formula, which is fine for now. (Be sure it's clear that the subtraction of $\dfrac{b}{2a}$ is outside the square–root sign.) The important thing is for students to see that there is a general process—in fact, a formula—that they can use to solve *any* quadratic equation (at least any quadratic equation with real roots). They will look at equations with complex roots more closely in *Imagine a Solution* and *Complex Numbers and Quadratic Equations*.

What About Two Roots?

Raise the issue that the equations students have the examining have generally had two solutions, even if only one made sense in the context, and ask where the other solution is. If this issue hasn't been raised yet, you might use a graph to illustrate why a quadratic function generally has two roots.

If needed, return to a numerical example to bring out that Step 5 is a bit subtler than just described. Help students to see that, in fact, there are two possibilities for the value of $x + \dfrac{b}{2a}$:

$$\sqrt{-\frac{c}{a} + \left(\frac{b}{2a}\right)^2} \quad \text{or} \quad -\sqrt{-\frac{c}{a} + \left(\frac{b}{2a}\right)^2}$$

You might suggest that students can write the pair of solutions with a single equation:

$$x = \pm\sqrt{-\frac{c}{a} + \left(\frac{b}{2a}\right)^2} - \frac{b}{2a}$$

Applying the Formula

Have students apply the formula to the equation from *Look Out Below!* That is, have them identify a, b, and c for the equation $200 - 30t - 10t^2 = 0$ and verify that the formula gives the same answers they found earlier.

Students might rewrite the equation as $10t^2 + 30t - 200 = 0$, but they can also use it as is, with $a = -10$, $b = -30$, and $c = 200$. Either approach gives $\frac{b}{2a} = 1.5$ [so $\left(\frac{b}{2a}\right)^2 = 2.25$] and $-\frac{c}{a} = 20$, and leads to $x = \pm\sqrt{22.25} - 1.5$. The positive square root equals 3.2, which answers the question from *Look Out Below!*

The Standard Quadratic Formula

Lead the class through the algebra of transforming their work into the standard version of the quadratic formula, or simply give them the standard version and tell them that it is equivalent to what they found. In either case, post the official result:

If $ax^2 + bx + c = 0$, and $a \neq 0$, then $x = \dfrac{-b \pm \sqrt{b^2 - 4ac}}{2a}$.

Tell the class that this equation, which gives the solution in terms of the coefficients, is called the **quadratic formula**.

You might point out that in this version of the formula, the various fractions have been combined into a single "master fraction" using a common denominator that is outside the square-root sign. You might have students verify this version of the formula using the equation from *Look Out Below!*

After this introduction, students can work on the activity. Caution them to be careful about parentheses when entering complicated expressions into their calculators.

Discussing and Debriefing the Activity

For Question 1, students should come up with $x = -4$ and $x = 7$ as solutions. Go over the details carefully, clarifying issues about signs and how to deal with the $\pm$ symbol. For instance, bring out that the coefficient b is -3, so the term $-b$ in the numerator is "positive three." (Students often think of $-b$ as "negative b" rather than as "the opposite of b" and may reason that if b is already negative, there is no need to change the sign.)

The expression inside the square-root sign comes out to 121, so students can eliminate the square root by recognizing that $\sqrt{121} = 11$. Help them see that they can rewrite the expression $\frac{3 \pm 11}{2}$ as two separate expressions, $\frac{3+11}{2}$ and $\frac{3-11}{2}$, and simplify to get 7 and -4. Have them verify that both values actually fit the equation. You might want to point out that this equation can be solved by factoring as well.

Then have students graph the function given by the equation $y = x^2 - 3x - 28$ and interpret the two solutions in terms of the graph. They should see that the graph crosses the x-axis at two places, $x = -4$ and $x = 7$, which are the points on the graph where $y = 0$.

For Question 2, students will need to put the equation in standard form. They should then be able to see that $a = 3$, $b = 7$, and $c = -5$. According to the quadratic formula, there are two solutions, given by the expression $\frac{-7 \pm \sqrt{109}}{6}$. This problem involves a value of a different from 1 and a different sign for b, so review the details of the solution.

Students may have some difficulty with the computation needed to check these exact answers. As a second check, they could use numerical approximations and see that these values are very nearly correct. This is another opportunity to reinforce the distinction between exact and approximate solutions.

Key Questions

Why do problems of this type lead to quadratic equations?
What might the general quadratic equation look like?
Where's the other solution?

Using Your ABCs

Intent

Students use the quadratic formula to solve problems.

Mathematics

Applying the quadratic formula to equations that arise from the context of a situation, students consider the significance of having two solutions. They are also introduced to the issue of the nonexistence of real solutions.

Progression

Students work individually to solve equations using the quadratic formula and then to write and solve quadratic equations for problem situations. The follow-up discussion focuses on the mechanics of applying the quadratic formula and examines the significance of an equation having no solution or two solutions.

Approximate Time

30 minutes for activity (at home or in class)
20 minutes for discussion

Classroom Organization

Individuals, followed by whole-class discussion

Doing the Activity

This activity requires little or no introduction.

Discussing and Debriefing the Activity

You can facilitate a smooth transition from this activity into the work with complex numbers (beginning with *Imagine a Solution*) by discussing Question 2 before Question 1.

Question 2

For the various parts of Question 2, students may make different choices about what their variables represent, which may lead to different equations. Have presenters show how to use the quadratic formula in each case to get exact solutions. If there are common errors, take time to discuss them. Be sure to talk about what the solution to each equation means in terms of the problem.

For part a, using x to represent the length of the shorter side leads to the equation $x(x + 5) = 126$. This is equivalent to $x^2 + 5x - 126 = 0$, which has $x = 9$ and $x = -14$ as solutions. If $x = 9$, the longer side of the rectangle is 14, and the rectangle is 9 feet by 14 feet.

Students should recognize that $x = -14$ does not make literal sense as a side length. They may also notice that this solution has the same absolute value as the long side and interpret this solution as representing a rectangle with sides whose "lengths" are -14 feet and -9 feet. Such a rectangle could be interpreted as lying in the third quadrant of a coordinate system, in which both x and y are negative.

If students set up their equations using the variable to represent the longer side of the rectangle, the equation and its solutions will be different, but the rectangle's dimensions will be the same.

For part b, if x represents the longer leg, the equation is $x^2 + (x - 6)^2 = 13^2$. In standard form, this is $2x^2 - 12x - 133 = 0$, and students can use the quadratic formula to get the two solutions $\dfrac{12 \pm \sqrt{1208}}{4}$, which yields approximately $x = -5.7$ and $x = 11.7$. Only one solution makes literal sense, and the triangle has legs of length 11.7 and 5.7. As with part a, students might give an interpretation to the negative solution and might set up the equation differently.

For part c, students should get the equation simply by setting the expression $90 + 50t - 16t^2$ equal to 120. In standard form, the equation is $16t^2 - 50t + 30 = 0$, which has two solutions, $\dfrac{50 \pm \sqrt{580}}{32}$. This yields values of approximately $t = 0.81$ and $t = 2.32$.

Before discussing whether both solutions make sense, ask, What does the equation $h = 90 + 50t - 16t^2$ mean in terms of the situation? Students will probably be able to interpret this as meaning that the object started with a height of 90 feet and an upward speed of 50 feet per second.

With this in mind, ask, Which of the solutions to the equation make sense in the problem? One solution ($t = 0.81$) indicates the time when the object reaches 120 feet on the way up. The other solution ($t = 2.32$) indicates the time when the object reaches 120 feet on the way down.

Interpreting the Negative Solution to "Look Out Below!"

After students have interpreted the two solutions to Question 2c in terms of the object going up and then down, you may want to return to *Look Out Below!*, in which the equation had two solutions, $t = 3.2$ and $t = -6.2$. If they did not come up with an interpretation then for the negative solution, you might ask whether it makes more sense now.

They might imagine that someone threw the pillow upward with just the right force so that it would pass Maxine on the way down at a speed of 30 feet per second. The solution $t = -6.2$ means the pillow would have to have been thrown upward 6.2 seconds before Maxine saw it. (As noted earlier, the issue of air resistance makes the mathematical model for this problem a poor one. That issue may also make this interpretation seem somewhat unrealistic.)

The General Height Formula

Ask students to develop a general formula for the height of a freely falling or rising object in terms of its initial height and velocity. They should come up with a principle like this one, which generalizes the similar statement from the discussion following *Free Fall*:

> **If a freely falling or rising object (straight down or up) has an initial height of h feet and an initial velocity of v feet per second (where a positive value for v means upward motion), its height after t seconds is $h + vt - 16t^2$ feet.**

Post this new principle for reference.

The Case v = 0

Ask students to compare the statement just developed with the principle posted for *Free Fall* giving the expression $h - 16t^2$ for the height of an object falling *from rest* from a height of h feet. They should see that the "from rest" formula, for the case $v = 0$, is a special case of the general formula. Remind them, if needed, that the initial velocity of the object in *Free Fall* was zero.

Question 1

Part a has integer solutions ($x = -3$ and $x = -4$), and students should be able to describe how they used the quadratic formula to get them.

Part b and c are a bit more difficult, because the exact solutions, given below, require square roots. You may need to caution students to pay particular attention to signs.

- Question 1b: $\dfrac{3+\sqrt{41}}{2}$ and $\dfrac{3-\sqrt{41}}{2}$, or approximately 4.7 and −1.7

- Question 1c: $\dfrac{-5+\sqrt{33}}{4}$ and $\dfrac{-5-\sqrt{33}}{4}$, or approximately 0.2 and −2.7

Part d presents a new challenge, because the equation has no real roots. Students should have found that the quadratic formula yields the expression $\frac{3 \pm \sqrt{-23}}{4}$.

Ask, **What does this expression mean?** Be sure students articulate that there is no number (that they know of) whose square is −23 and that this means the equation has no solutions (within the number system as they probably know it so far).

Also ask, **What does this lack of a solution mean in terms of the graph of** $y = 2x^2 - 3x + 4$**?** Students should be able to articulate that the graph has no x-intercepts and give a rough sketch of what such a graph might look like. (It's sufficient if they merely sketch a parabola opening upward that is entirely above the x-axis.) Students might want to verify, using their calculators, that the graph of $y = 2x^2 - 3x + 4$ has no x-intercepts.

Key Questions

What does the equation $h = 90 + 50t - 16t^2$ **mean in terms of the situation?**
Which of the solutions to the equation make sense in the problem?
What does this lack of a solution mean in terms of the graph of $y = 2x^2 - 3x + 4$**?**

Imagine a Solution

Intent

This activity introduces imaginary numbers.

Mathematics

Students saw in Question 1d of *Using Your ABCs* that some quadratic equations have no real solutions, as evidenced by a negative radicand when they apply the quadratic formula. This new activity introduces i as the square root of -1.

Progression

Students work on the activity individually or in groups and then discuss their discoveries.

Approximate Time

30 minutes

Classroom Organization

Individuals or small groups, followed by whole-class discussion

Doing the Activity

Tell students that in the next two activities, they will learn about two new kinds of numbers: **imaginary numbers** and **complex numbers**. These new numbers will enable them to solve equations that don't seem to have any solutions.

You might introduce the topic by asking for the simplest quadratic function students can create that has no x–intercepts. They may generate such functions as $f(x) = x^2 + k$ with $k > 0$, which lead to seemingly impossible equations like $x^2 + k = 0$. To resolve the dilemma, students could then read the explanation in the student book.

As students work through the questions, you might clarify that an expression like $2i$ is shorthand for $2 \cdot i$. In this respect, i is treated as a variable rather than as a number.

You might also give an example of multiplication with imaginary numbers, such as rewriting $2i \cdot 3i$ as $2 \cdot 3 \cdot i \cdot i$ and then simplifying, first as $6i^2$ and finally as -6.

Discussing and Debriefing the Activity

For Question 1, ask students how they could multiply to check their solutions. You might note that each problem has two answers and that neither is the "positive" square root.

For Question 2c, you may need to reassure students that they can rewrite a negative radicand like $\sqrt{-5}$ as the product $\sqrt{5} \cdot \sqrt{-1}$.

For Question 3, students should see that the powers of i form a repeating pattern with a cycle of length 4. For part c, they might articulate the process of dividing the exponent by 4 and finding the remainder.

Complex Numbers and Quadratic Equations

Intent

Students' work with imaginary numbers is extended to include the full system of complex numbers.

Mathematics

Students see that a combination of a real and an imaginary number is needed to express the solutions to some quadratic equations, and that these complex numbers are typically expressed in the form $a + bi$.

Progression

Students work on the activity individually and share discoveries in a class discussion.

Approximate Time

25 minutes for activity (at home or in class)
10 to 15 minutes for discussion

Classroom Organization

Individuals, followed by whole-class discussion

Doing the Activity

Tell students they are about to encounter a system of numbers called the **complex numbers,** a system that includes both the imaginary numbers and the real numbers (the numbers represented on the number line). You may want to have students read the explanation in the student book and ask questions for clarification before they tackle the activity.

Discussing and Debriefing the Activity

Question 1 involves substitution, the distributive property, and the definition of i. Students might use an area diagram similar to those they have seen for squaring binomials to find that $(1 + i)^2$ is equal to $1 + 2i + (-1)$, or simply $2i$.

1   i

1   1   i

i   i i^2

This gives $(1 + i)^2 - 2(1 + i) + 2 = 2i - (2 + 2i) + 2 = 0$.

In Question 2, substituting into the quadratic formula (with $a = 1$, $b = -2$, and $c = 2$) yields the expression $\dfrac{2 \pm \sqrt{(-2)^2 - 4 \cdot 1 \cdot 2}}{2}$, which simplifies to $\dfrac{2 \pm \sqrt{-4}}{2}$. Students should see that $\sqrt{-4}$ is equal to $2i$ and then simplify the fraction to $1 \pm i$.

For Question 3, they need only substitute $1 - i$ for x.

For Question 4, they will have to use radical multiplication to separate $\sqrt{-12}$ into $\sqrt{4} \cdot \sqrt{3} \cdot \sqrt{-1}$.

Supplemental Activities

Complex Conjugation (extension) introduces the complex conjugate, how it is used in the division of complex numbers, and how it arises in solving quadratic equations.

Absolutely Complex (extension) explores the absolute value of a complex number.

Complex Components

Intent

Students explore the representation and addition of complex numbers on the complex plane using vectors.

Mathematics

By examining the representation of two complex numbers and their sum as vectors in the complex plane, students discover that vectors can be added graphically by moving one vector so that it begins where the other ends. Students will notice that the real and imaginary parts of the two numbers being added are treated separately, much like the vertical and horizontal components of velocity will be treated in the unit problem. (The polar form of complex numbers is introduced and explored in the supplemental activities *The Polar Complex* and *Polar Roots.*)

Progression

Students work on the activity individually and share their findings with the class.

Approximate Time

30 minutes

Classroom Organization

Individuals, followed by whole-class discussion

Doing the Activity

Introduce the activity by explaining that the class will now start considering the fact that the diver is already moving at the moment he is released.

Discussing and Debriefing the Activity

Questions 1 and 2 should be straightforward.

Have two or three students present their answers to Question 3, and ask others to contribute any other ways they might have proceeded. The point is to review three distinct ways of constructing the vector representing the sum 4 + 5i:

- Have the vector for 1 + 4i begin where the vector for 3 + i ends, moving the second vector so that its length and direction do not change.
- Follow the same procedure by starting with the vector for 1 + 4i.

- Notice that the four points form a parallelogram and that the "sum vector" is a particular diagonal of the parallelogram.

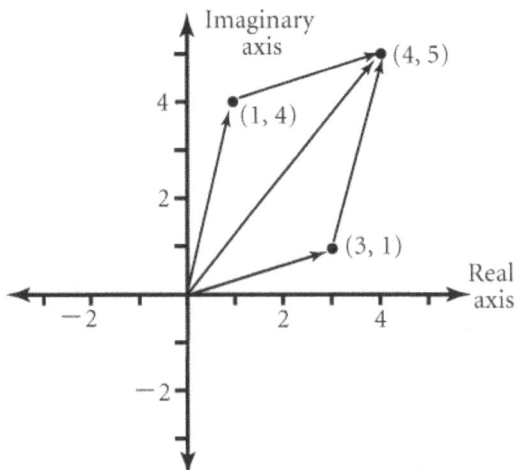

Also point out that diagonal vectors can be added in the same way as complex numbers, that is, by adding their horizontal (real) components and their vertical (imaginary) components separately.

Follow up this discussion by asking, What are the key characteristics of a vector? The goal is to develop an intuitive understanding that in a two-dimensional geometric context, a vector

- is a line segment
- has a fixed length
- has a fixed orientation (that is, a fixed angle with regard to some reference direction)
- has a fixed direction (that is, it begins at one end and ends at the other)
- can be moved to any position in the plane as long as its length, orientation, and direction remain the same

Conclude by telling students that later in the unit, they will use vectors to represent velocities for the diver on the Ferris wheel.

Key Question

What are the key characteristics of a vector?

Supplemental Activities

The Polar Complex (extension) introduces the polar form of a complex number.

Polar Roots (extension) has students use the polar form to find and test roots of complex numbers.

Number Research (extension) asks students to research the names given to different sets of numbers and to make a poster illustrating their findings.

Three O'Clock Drop

Intent

After the interlude with complex numbers, students now return to the main topic and examine a situation in which a falling diver has initial upward motion.

Mathematics

The opening discussion introduces the distinction between velocity and speed and establishes the convention that vertically upward motion will be described as having a positive velocity. Students then use this convention in evaluating a Ferris wheel situation in which the diver has initial upward motion.

Progression

The teacher introduces this activity by discussing the fact that velocity involves both a speed and a direction and the convention that positive velocity in the vertical direction means upward motion.

Approximate Time

10 minutes for introduction
25 minutes for activity (at home or in class)
10 to 20 minutes for discussion

Classroom Organization

Individuals, preceded and followed by whole-class discussion

Doing the Activity

Have the class compare the height equations from the last several problems:

- $h = 200 - 30t - 10t^2$ for *Look Out Below!*
- $h = 65 - 7.85t - 16t^2$ for *Big Push*
- $h = 90 + 50t - 16t^2$ for Question 2c of *Using Your ABCs*

Bring out that in Question 2c of *Using Your ABCs,* the coefficient of *t* is positive, while in the other problems, it is negative. Ask, What does the sign of the coefficient of *t* say about the situation? Students will probably recognize that in Question 2c, the object was going up to begin with, while in the other problems, the object was going down initially.

In the context of vertical motion, it usually makes sense to think of "up" as the positive direction. Tell students that they should use this convention for the remainder of the unit.

With this convention in mind, return to the three problems and ask, **Why does the coefficient of the linear term in the height function have the sign it does in each case?** Help students reach these conclusions:

- In *Look Out Below!,* the pillow had a velocity of –30 feet per second when Maxine first saw it.
- In *Big Push,* the diver had a velocity of –7.85 feet per second when he was first released from the Ferris wheel.
- In Question 2c of *Using Your ABCs,* the object had an initial velocity of 50 feet per second.

Velocity Has Sign

Tell students that **velocity** is the term used in physics to indicate the combination of speed and direction. Thus, the velocity of an object tells both the speed at which the object is traveling and the direction of the motion. Velocity may be positive or negative, but speed is never negative—in fact, it's the absolute value of velocity.

Acceleration and the Sign of Velocity

There is potential for confusion about the idea of constant acceleration in a context in which the sign of the velocity is changing. We have established the convention that positive velocity represents upward motion. While an object is moving upward, the effect of gravity is to slow it down, decreasing its speed. On the other hand, when an object is moving downward, the effect of gravity is to increase its speed.

Discussing and Debriefing the Activity

For Question 1, students will probably develop an equation for the time the diver is falling from a formula for an object's height in terms of time. They might simply write down this equation, based on earlier examples, without going through the analysis of finding the average velocity.

The diver's height t seconds after release is given by the expression $65 + 7.85t - 16t^2$. As a follow-up to the discussion of the sign convention for velocity, ask why this expression is identical to that for *Big Push* except for the sign of the coefficient of t. Students should see that the diver is being released from the Ferris wheel at the same height and with the same speed in both cases. The distinction is that here his initial motion is upward, while in *Big Push* it was downward.

To answer Question 1, students need to determine when the diver is 8 feet off the ground, so they need to solve the equation $65 + 7.85t - 16t^2 = 8$. The solutions to the equation are $t \approx 2.15$ and $t \approx -1.66$. Encourage students to use the quadratic formula to get the exact values in terms of square roots. (In *Falling Time for*

Vertical Motion, they will need to use the formula to get a general expression for the falling time of a free-falling object.)

You might discuss once again that the equation only imperfectly represents the problem, because only one of its solutions makes sense in this context.

For Question 2, students might simply substitute 57 for h in the expression $\sqrt{\dfrac{h}{16}}$ (using the expression developed in Question 4 of *Free Fall*). Or they might point out that the time is the same as that for Question 3 of *Big Push,* namely, $t \approx 1.89$. Students can also find this value by solving the equation obtained by eliminating the term $7.85t$ from the equation used in Question 1; that is, by solving $65 - 16t^2 = 8$.

Next, ask, How much of a difference does the diver's upward motion from the movement of the Ferris wheel make in his falling time? Students can calculate that it takes approximately an additional 0.26 second. You might compare this to the decrease in falling time resulting from the effect of the Ferris wheel's motion in *Big Push,* which was approximately 0.23 second. Although the amounts are roughly the same, they are not identical.

Key Questions

What does the sign of the coefficient of t say about the situation?
Why does the coefficient of the linear term in the height function have the sign it does?
How much of a difference does the diver's upward motion from the movement of the Ferris wheel make in his falling time?

Up, Down, Splat!

Intent

Students continue to work with a falling body having an initial upward motion.

Mathematics

This activity puts initial upward motion in a different context. As in *Three O'Clock Drop*, students need to recognize that they can find the time until the object hits the ground by setting the height variable to zero and solving the resulting quadratic equation. In this activity, they are also asked the object's speed at the moment of impact, which can be found by using the initial velocity, falling time, and acceleration.

Progression

Students work on the activity individually or in groups and share findings in a class discussion.

Approximate Time

15 minutes for activity (at home or in class)
10 to 15 minutes for discussion

Classroom Organization

Individuals or small groups, followed by whole-class discussion

Doing the Activity

This activity requires little or no introduction.

Discussing and Debriefing the Activity

Question 1 involves essentially the same process as used in the discussion of *Three O' Clock Drop*, but with different numbers. The height is given by the expression $25 + 35t - 16t^2$, and the solutions to the equation $25 + 35t - 16t^2 = 0$ are $t \approx 2.75$ and $t \approx -0.57$. Students presumably will recognize that the solution $t \approx 2.75$ is the one they want.

You might take this opportunity to make sure students are connecting their algebra to the situation by asking, What does the value 2.75 represent? They should see that it gives the number of seconds from when Melissa throws the egg container upward until it hits the ground.

Question 2 brings up an issue that has not yet been discussed in this sequence of problems: speed at impact. The simplest approach is to use the fact that velocity is decreasing by 32 feet per second for each second, so velocity after t seconds is given by the expression $35 - 32t$. Students can then substitute $t \approx 2.75$ into this expression to get a value of about -53 feet per second for the velocity when the egg container hits the ground. Be sure to discuss the significance of the negative sign.

Key Question

What does the value 2.75 represent?

Falling Time for Vertical Motion

Intent

Students use the quadratic formula to develop a general expression for the falling time of an object in terms of its initial velocity upward or downward and its initial height.

Mathematics

In the discussion of *Using Your ABCs*, students determined that the height of a freely falling object after t seconds is defined by the expression $h + vt - 16t^2$. Now they will use that information to derive an expression for the falling time in terms of h and v. That is, they will use the quadratic formula to solve the equation $h + vt - 16t^2 = 0$ for t.

Progression

Students work on the activity individually or in groups. The follow-up discussion includes an exploration of whether the expression that students develop is consistent with that developed earlier for a body falling from rest. This exploration provides a nice review of simplifying radical expressions.

Approximate Time

5 minutes for introduction
20 to 25 minutes for activity (at home or in class)
10 to 15 minutes for discussion

Classroom Organization

Individuals or small groups, followed by whole-class discussion

Doing the Activity

Little or no introduction is needed for this activity.

Discussing and Debriefing the Activity

For Questions 1 and 2, students should rewrite the equation, likely as $16t^2 - vt - h = 0$, and then apply the quadratic formula, to get

$$t = \frac{v \pm \sqrt{(-v)^2 - 4 \cdot 16 \cdot (-h)}}{32}$$

which simplifies to

$$t = \frac{v \pm \sqrt{v^2 + 64h}}{32}$$

The task in Question 3 is to decide which sign to use. Students may tap their experience with previous problems, or they may be able to analyze the situation. For example, because h is assumed to be positive, the expression inside the square-root sign is greater than v^2, so using the negative sign would result in a negative value for t.

Post this solution, with a description of what it represents:

> **If an object is put into the air with an initial vertical velocity of v feet per second and falls a net distance of h feet, the time for this fall is given by the expression**
>
> $$\frac{v + \sqrt{v^2 + 64h}}{32}$$

Explain that *net distance* is the distance from the object's initial position to the ground. You might bring out that this expression is smaller if v is negative than if v is positive with the same absolute value. That is, the object will reach the ground faster if it is initially moving downward.

What if $v = 0$?

This complex expression may intimidate students. One way to make it less mysterious, as well as to review previous ideas, is to ask, What does this expression say about the case $v = 0$? That is, does this expression agree with what students learned earlier about objects falling from rest?

Let students investigate this question for a few minutes. Their first step should be to replace v with 0, which simplifies the expression considerably. But they may not immediately connect the resulting expression, $\frac{\sqrt{64h}}{32}$, with their earlier result, $\sqrt{\frac{h}{16}}$.

Have groups examine whether these two expressions are equivalent. If they get stuck, you might ask whether they can write $\frac{\sqrt{64h}}{32}$ as simply a radical or whether they can write $\sqrt{\frac{h}{16}}$ with a radical in the numerator only. In other words, Are the expressions $\frac{\sqrt{64h}}{32}$ and $\sqrt{\frac{h}{16}}$ equivalent? Another option is to square and then simplify both expressions and see that the results are the same.

Key Questions

What does this expression say about the case $v = 0$?

Are the expressions $\dfrac{\sqrt{64h}}{32}$ and $\sqrt{\dfrac{h}{16}}$ equivalent?

Components of Velocity

Intent

In these activities, students learn to work with falling motion that is not purely vertical.

Mathematics

Up to this point, students have considered falling motion in which the initial velocity was nonexistent, vertically upward, or vertically downward. Unless the diver is released at the 3 o'clock or 9 o'clock positions, however, he will have an initial velocity that is not purely vertical.

In these activities, students will learn that the diver's motion can be split into two components, vertical and horizontal velocity. These two components can be calculated separately: the diver falls as if he were not moving horizontally, and moves horizontally as if he were not falling. The two components are tied together only in that the horizontal motion is limited by the falling time.

Progression

The analysis begins with a pair of activities in which the initial motion is purely horizontal, one involving the Ferris wheel (*High Noon*) and one set in a different context (*Leap of Faith*). Then students look at another pair of activities (*The Ideal Skateboard* and *Racing the River*) where the initial velocity is neither purely vertical nor purely horizontal, but in which they do not have to deal with the complication posed by acceleration due to gravity as they determine and work with the velocity's horizontal and vertical components. In *One O'Clock Without Gravity,* they apply this idea to the Ferris wheel.

Swimming Pointers and *Vector Velocities* extend students' brief introduction to vectors (in *Complex Components*) to vertical and horizontal components of velocity. Students combine the two components to find the resultant and also resolve a given vector into components.

Students return to the Ferris wheel with a group of activities (*One O'Clock Without Gravity*, *Velocities on the Wheel*, *Release at Any Angle*, and *Moving Diver at Two O'Clock*) that get them ready to complete the unit problem. *An Expanded Portfolio of Formulas* is, in a sense, the follow-up to Part I of *A Simple Summary and a Complex Beginning*.

Finally, in *The Danger of Simplification*, students explore whether it was really necessary to consider the effect of the diver's initial motion.

High Noon
Leap of Faith

The Ideal Skateboard
Racing the River
One O'Clock Without Gravity
Swimming Pointers
Vector Velocities
Velocities on the Wheel
Release at Any Angle
An Expanded Portfolio of Formulas
Moving Diver at Two O'Clock
The Danger of Simplification

High Noon

Intent

Students begin to consider the motion of falling objects that have a horizontal component to the initial velocity.

Mathematics

It often surprises students to realize that horizontal motion does not affect the length of time it takes an object to fall. This realization can then lead to confusion over the fact that the horizontal motion, on the other hand, is limited by the falling time. The horizontal and vertical components of falling motion can be treated completely separately, but the vertical motion must be analyzed first to determine the length of time the object will be moving horizontally.

Progression

The teacher introduces this activity with a brief discussion of what needs to come next in solving the main unit problem. Once students realize that the Ferris wheel will almost certainly impart an initial horizontal motion to the diver, discussion continues with an observation that horizontal motion and gravitational fall work independently of each other. Students then work through the activity individually or in groups, and the class reviews the findings.

Approximate Time

35 to 40 minutes

Classroom Organization

Individuals or small groups, preceded and followed by whole-class discussion

Doing the Activity

Now that the class has dealt with the falling motion of a body having vertical initial motion, ask, **What do you think comes next in the solution of the unit problem?** Point out that in the 3 o'clock and 9 o'clock positions, the diver's initial motion either shortens or lengthens the time it takes him to fall to the water level (as compared to the time it would take if he fell from rest).

Tell students to suppose now that the diver is released at some position other than 3 o'clock or 9 o'clock. Ask, **What other effect might the motion of the Ferris wheel have on the diver, besides shortening or lengthening the time of his fall?** Students should recognize that he would also be moving to one side or the other and that this would cause him to land in a different place than if he were dropped from rest. Tell students that the next aspect of the unit is to learn how to combine this sideways motion with vertical motion.

Horizontal Motion and Gravitational Fall Are Independent

Before dealing with these other cases of the unit problem, students need to learn one more principle about the physics of motion.

Explain that the key idea for combining horizontal and vertical motion is to treat them completely separately. Acknowledge that this principle may not fit students' intuition, but explain that it can be verified experimentally. You might summarize and post the principle as follows:

> **If an object is moving sideways as it falls, then**
> - **the rate at which its height changes is the same as if it were falling straight down**
> - **the rate at which it moves sideways is the same as if there were no gravity**

Bring out that the object's overall speed is a blend of the vertical and horizontal speeds and is greater than either of these separate speeds. (The term used in physics for this combined motion is *resultant*.)

Discussing and Debriefing the Activity

If the class has already discussed *Leap of Faith,* you may wish to give groups more time to work on this activity. This will give you an opportunity to determine whether the presentation of this activity will be fruitful for the whole class or will simply be a repetition of the ideas in the earlier discussion.

At the 12 o'clock position, the diver is 107 feet above the water level, so his falling time (down to the water level) is $\sqrt{\frac{107}{16}} \approx 2.59$ seconds. His horizontal speed at the moment of release is 7.85 ft/s, so he will travel $7.85 \cdot 2.59 \approx 20.3$ feet to the left as he falls.

Key Questions

What do you think comes next in the solution of the unit problem?
What other effect might the motion of the Ferris wheel have on the diver besides shortening or lengthening the time of his fall?

Leap of Faith

Intent

Students continue to analyze falling motion for a body having an initial horizontal velocity.

Mathematics

This activity applies the ideas from *High Noon* in a context other than the Ferris wheel.

Progression

Students work on the activity individually. The follow-up discussion emphasizes that an object's falling time can be found independently of its horizontal motion.

Approximate Time

25 to 30 minutes for activity (at home or in class)
10 minutes for discussion

Classroom Organization

Individuals, followed by whole-class discussion

Doing the Activity

This activity requires little or no introduction.

Discussing and Debriefing the Activity

The key to this activity is to recognize, based upon the ideas in the discussion introducing *High Noon*, that the falling time in this situation is the same as that for an object falling 30 feet from rest: $\sqrt{\dfrac{30}{16}}$ seconds, or about 1.37 seconds.

By applying that previous discussion's second principle, students will see that the jumper will cover the same horizontal distance as if he or she had continued moving horizontally at a constant rate. The task is to find that rate. Because the jumper wants to travel 15 feet in 1.37 seconds, the appropriate rate is $\dfrac{15}{1.37}$ ft/s, or about 11 ft/s.

Question 2 addresses an interesting side issue. If the net is 10 feet across, the jumper can travel anywhere from 10 feet to 20 feet and still land in the net (although it's probably best to land somewhere near the middle). Therefore, the jumper's initial speed can be as little as $\frac{10}{1.37}$ ft/s (about 7.3 ft/s) and as much as $\frac{20}{1.37}$ ft/s (about 14.6 ft/s).

The Ideal Skateboard

Intent

Students analyze velocity in terms of its vertical and horizontal components in a context that does not involve the complication of gravity.

Mathematics

Until this point, students have worked with initial velocities that are either purely horizontal or purely vertical. In *High Noon*, the combination of the horizontal initial velocity and the vertical pull of gravity resulted in motion that was both horizontal and vertical. Students are now reassured that they can always split motion into perpendicular components for separate treatment, enabling them to work with situations in which the initial motion is neither purely horizontal nor purely vertical.

Progression

The teacher introduces this activity with a discussion of the principle that velocities can always be broken into perpendicular components that can be analyzed separately. Students then work through the activity individually or in groups, and the class reviews the findings.

Approximate Time

40 to 50 minutes

Classroom Organization

Individuals or small groups, preceded and followed by whole-class discussion

Doing the Activity

Ask students to list the specific cases of the diver's release that they have looked at.

- The 9 o'clock position, in *Big Push*
- The 3 o'clock position, in *Three O'Clock Drop*
- The 12 o'clock position, in *High Noon*

Ask, What is special about these cases? Someone will probably recognize that these are all situations in which the diver's initial velocity is either purely vertical or purely horizontal.

Remind students that in *High Noon*, although the diver's initial velocity was horizontal, his overall movement was both vertical and horizontal. How did you work with this combination of horizontal motion and the downward force of gravity? Students should be able to articulate that they treated the two parts of the diver's motion separately, using these two principles:

- The diver moves sideways as if there were no gravity.
- The diver moves down as if there were no sideways motion.

Review that according to both theoretical and experimental physics, we can always treat these two parts of motion as if they were completely separate. Introduce the phrases *vertical component of velocity* and *horizontal component of velocity* for these two parts of an object's motion.

Go over how this idea works in the context of *High Noon*. Ask, What was the vertical component of the diver's velocity 1 second after he was released? What was the horizontal component? Students should see that the vertical component would be the same as if he had fallen from rest, −32 ft/s. (This velocity is negative because he is moving downward.) The horizontal component doesn't change during the diver's fall, so it is the same as when he started, −7.85 ft/s. (This velocity is negative because he is moving to the left.)

Make sure students realize that for the vertical component, they need to be thinking about instantaneous velocity, because this component is changing at each second. You might point out that this change in the vertical component explains why the diver's path gets steeper as he falls.

For Question 2, you might remind students that the skateboarder's path is tangent to the circle, meaning it is perpendicular to the circle's "2 o'clock" radius.

Discussing and Debriefing the Activity

Question 1 is like a similar question for the Ferris wheel. The skateboarder's speed is approximately 7.33 ft/s.

Question 2 contains an important element: the determination of the angle. Students may find it helpful to use a diagram of an overhead view of the situation, like this one:

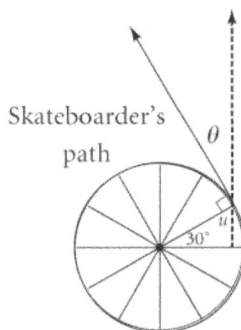

One way to find angle θ is to first find angle u and then solve the equation $u + 90° + \theta = 180°$ (which uses the fact that the tangent is perpendicular to the radius). Once students see that θ is 30°, mention that it's no coincidence that θ is equal to the angle made between the radius to the 3 o'clock position and the radius to the point of release.

Students might then use a diagram like the next one to see that the skateboarder moves 7.33 cos 30° feet, or approximately 6.35 feet, closer to the wall each second. Identify this as the "toward-the-wall" component of the skateboarder's velocity.

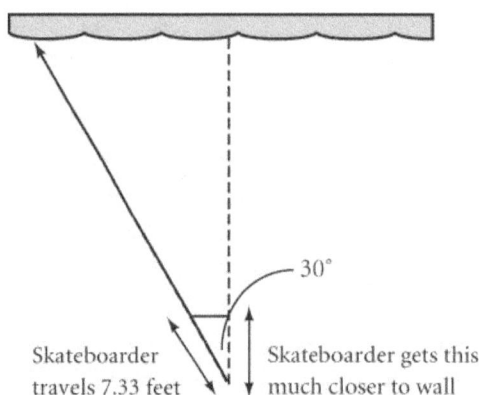

Students will probably answer Question 4 by dividing the distance (30 feet) by the toward-the-wall velocity component (6.35 ft/s). This gives a time of approximately 4.7 seconds for the skateboarder to reach the wall.

Question 5 is intended as a confirmation of the component concept. Students should see that the total distance d that the skateboarder travels fits the equation $\cos 30° = \dfrac{30}{d}$, so $d = \dfrac{30}{\cos 30°} \approx 34.6$ feet. Dividing this result by 7.33 ft/s again gives about 4.7 seconds.

Whichever way students find this time, point out that cos 30° is part of the computation. The computation for Question 4 is $\dfrac{30}{7.33 \cos 30°}$, while the computation for Question 5 is

$$\dfrac{\left(\dfrac{30}{\cos 30°}\right)}{7.33}$$

Now have students find the "parallel-to-the-wall" component of the skateboarder's velocity. They will probably see that in magnitude, this component is 7.33 sin θ ft/s. You might use the small triangle in the diagram above to point out that because the two components are perpendicular, they and the overall speed satisfy the Pythagorean theorem. That is, the values satisfy the equation $(7.33 \sin \theta)^2 + (7.33 \cos \theta)^2 = 7.33^2$.

Key Questions

What is special about these cases (the 3, 9, and 12 o'clock drops)?
How did you work with this combination of horizontal motion and the downward force of gravity?
What was the vertical component of the *High Noon* diver's velocity 1 second after he was released? What was the horizontal component?

Racing the River

Intent

Students express velocity in terms of horizontal and vertical components.

Mathematics

This activity, which is quite similar to *The Ideal Skateboard,* poses a situation in which two swimmers are racing across a river, one swimming straight across and the other at an angle to the shoreline. Students need to recognize that the speed of the swimmer who is crossing at an angle can be broken into two components: one perpendicular to the shoreline and one parallel to the shoreline. The activity presents the same situation with two different angles so that students can observe that each of the two perpendicular components of the speed is affected by the angle.

Progression

Students work on the activity individually or in groups, followed by a class discussion.

Approximate Time

30 minutes for activity (at home or in class)
10 minutes for discussion

Classroom Organization

Individuals or small groups, followed by whole-class discussion

Materials

Transparency of *Racing the River* blackline master

Doing the Activity

You may want to clarify that students are to assume there is no river current in this situation.

Discussing and Debriefing the Activity

The key idea here is recognizing that a River High swimmer's speed has a "toward-shore" component that depends on the angle at which the swimmer is moving.

Questions 1 and 2

These questions should be fairly straightforward. Students can find the distance for the River High swimmer using either the Pythagorean theorem or trigonometry. This distance (approximately 283 meters) can then be divided by the swimmer's speed (1.5 m/s) to get the time it will take the swimmer to finish the race (approximately 189 seconds). For Question 2, students will probably divide the distance by the time to get the rate (200 m ÷ 189 s ≈ 1.06 m/s).

Once the rate for the New High swimmer has been determined, get at the idea of the River High swimmer's toward-shore component with a pair of questions like these: How far from the starting shore is the New High swimmer after 50 seconds? How far from the starting shore is the River High swimmer after 50 seconds?

The first question can be answered by multiplying the New High swimmer's rate (1.06 m/s) by 50 seconds. Help students see that the second question must have the same answer as the first. Use that observation to establish that the River High swimmer is swimming toward the shore at a speed of 1.06 m/s, even though he is actually swimming at 1.5 m/s. Identify this value, 1.06 m/s, as the "toward-shore" component of the River High swimmer's speed.

Question 3

Question 3 is essentially a repeat of Questions 1 and 2, with a different angle. The goal is to elicit the idea that for a given speed, the toward-shore component of the River High swimmer's rate depends on the angle at which the swimmer is moving. You can illustrate this idea using a transparency of the diagram by placing a ruler along the starting shore and moving it gradually toward the finishing shore.

The activity *Swimming Pointers* will revisit this question, using vector diagrams to represent the toward-shore and parallel-to-shore components of the swimmer's velocity.

Key Questions

How far from the starting shore is the New High swimmer after 50 seconds?
How far from the starting shore is the River High swimmer after 50 seconds?

One O'Clock Without Gravity

Intent

Students find the vertical and horizontal components of velocity at a particular point on the Ferris wheel.

Mathematics

The Ideal Skateboard and *Racing the River* introduced students to the concept of breaking a speed into perpendicular components. Now they apply this to a simple case of the Ferris wheel situation, under the simplifying assumption that there is no gravity. The activity asks what the vertical and horizontal components of the diver's initial speed would be if he were released from the wheel at the 1 o'clock position, which requires students to determine the angle of the diver's initial motion at that clock position.

Progression

The activity is introduced with a brief discussion of how the angle of release might affect the diver's motion. Students then work on the activity individually or in groups. The follow-up discussion brings out that the angle between the diver's path and the vertical direction is equal to the angle through which the Ferris wheel turns before the diver is released.

Approximate Time

15 minutes for activity (at home or in class)
10 minutes for discussion

Classroom Organization

Individuals or small groups, followed by whole-class discussion

Doing the Activity

In Question 2 of *The Ideal Skateboard*, students found the angle (labeled θ) between the skateboarder's path and a perpendicular to the wall. Ask, How does an angle like θ figure into the Ferris wheel problem? Bring out that the diver's release point determines the angle of his initial motion, so it affects the way his motion breaks up into vertical and horizontal components. (You might raise the idea that his initial speed is the same no matter when he is released. Similarly, students could find the skateboarder's speed without first finding θ.)

With this introduction, have students work on the activity.

Discussing and Debriefing the Activity

Have volunteers share their ideas. The key to the problem is recognizing that the angle between the diver's path and the vertical direction (labeled θ in the diagram) is the same as the angle through which the diver has turned, which is the angle between the horizontal radius and the radius to his release point. (That angle of turn is 60°, because the diver is released at the 1 o'clock position.) The reasoning is the same as in *The Ideal Skateboard*, and you might again note that the angle between the path and the vertical is the same as the angle between the radius and the horizontal.

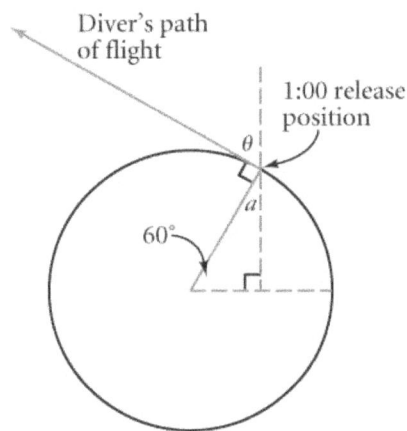

Diver's path
of flight

1:00 release
position

θ

a

60°

Once students find angle θ, the work is similar to what they did in *The Ideal Skateboard*. They might use a diagram like the next one to find the components.

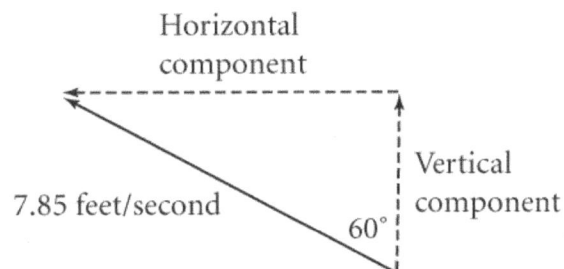

Horizontal
component

7.85 feet/second

Vertical
component

60°

Students should see that the vertical component has a magnitude of 7.85 cos 60°, so the diver is rising at about 3.9 ft/s. The horizontal component has a magnitude of 7.85 sin 60°, so the diver is moving to the left at about 6.8 ft/s.

Ask, **How do we show that horizontal travel is to the left or right?** Students should recognize that this horizontal motion is to the left, so the horizontal component of velocity is –6.8 ft/s.

You may want to save the values for these components of velocity for comparison with the results from Question 1 of *Velocities on the Wheel.*

Key Questions

How does an angle like θ figure into the Ferris wheel problem?

How do we show that horizontal travel is to the left or right?

Swimming Pointers

Intent

Students express a velocity vector as a vector sum of its vertical and horizontal components.

Mathematics

This activity recasts Question 3 from *Racing the River* in the context of vectors, which students first encountered in *Complex Components*. Students use vector diagrams and terminology together with trigonometry to resolve a vector into its vertical and horizontal components and then show how these combine to reconstruct the original vector.

Progression

Students work on the activity individually or in groups and share findings in a class discussion.

Approximate Time

15 minutes for activity (at home or in class)
10 minutes for discussion

Classroom Organization

Individuals or small groups, followed by whole-class discussion

Doing the Activity

This activity requires little or no introduction.

Discussing and Debriefing the Activity

Discussion of Questions 1 and 2 can be fairly brief. In Question 1a, the toward-shore component can be found by multiplying the overall speed by cos θ, where θ is the angle between the actual path and the direct route. That is, for each 1.5 meters the swimmer moves at an angle θ from the direct route, he or she gets closer to shore by 1.5 cos θ meters. You might have students consider the special cases $\theta = 0°$ and $\theta = 90°$ to confirm this result.

The main point of Question 3 is the vector diagram. Use this opportunity to review the various ways of constructing a diagram to show a vector sum. Students will probably construct a right triangle showing the tail of one component affixed to the head of the other. Ask, Does it matter which vector you use first in the diagram for adding two vectors? Students should be able to create two congruent triangles, thus suggesting that vector addition is commutative. Also bring out that the vector representing the sum of two other vectors can be seen as the diagonal of a rectangle, as in this diagram.

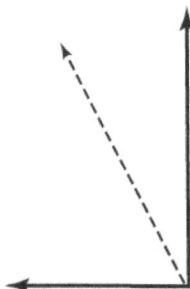

This is a more specific case of the sum of any two vectors (not necessarily perpendicular) being the diagonal of a parallelogram, which students found in *Complex Components*. If the vertical and horizontal velocity components are rounded to the nearest hundredth (1.30 and 0.75 m/s, respectively), the Pythagorean theorem gives 1.50 m/s for the resultant. The next activity, *Vector Velocities*, will generalize these results for any vector pointing northeast.

Key Question

Does it matter which vector you use first in the diagram for adding two vectors?

Vector Velocities

Intent

Students generalize their work in decomposing vectors and then develop the reverse process in the first-quadrant case.

Mathematics

Students develop a general procedure for finding the vertical and horizontal components of any vector featuring an acute angle in standard position. After considering a specific case based on a Ferris wheel, they generalize the reverse process of finding the magnitude and direction of a northeast-pointing vector given its horizontal and vertical components.

Progression

Students work on the activity in groups and share discoveries in a class discussion. In the next activity, *Velocities on the Wheel*, they explore vector decomposition for angles in any quadrant in the context of the Ferris wheel unit problem.

Approximate Time

30 to 40 minutes

Classroom Organization

Small groups, followed by whole-class discussion

Doing the Activity

This activity should need no introduction. Question 1b may stump some students who don't think to factor out *v* or don't recall the Pythagorean identity from trigonometry.

Students have solved problems like Questions 2 and 3 using triangles but not with vectors. Suggesting that they draw accurate diagrams should help those having trouble.

Question 2c is the most difficult, requiring first some angle matching and then some sort of proportion to convert degrees into hours and minutes.

Discussing and Debriefing the Activity

Have a student present Question 1, including a diagram. For part a, you might ask, *Do we know whether the same formulas will work for angles in other* quadrants? (No, we don't yet know; this is one focus of the next activity.) For part b, ask, **For what angles θ is $\sin^2 \theta + \cos^2 \theta = 1$ a true statement?** Be sure students recall that the identity works for all angles θ.

Question 2 involves some new ideas. In part a, the Pythagorean theorem yields exactly 6.5 feet per second. For part b, students will probably evaluate $\cos^{-1}\left(\dfrac{2.5}{6.5}\right)$ to get 67.4°, though some may use the inverse sine to find the complementary angle, or even the inverse tangent. Encourage students to give a clear description of the direction, not just to name an angle.

Part c involves reasoning about angles similar to that in *The Ideal Skateboard*. A diagram, such as this one, is essential:

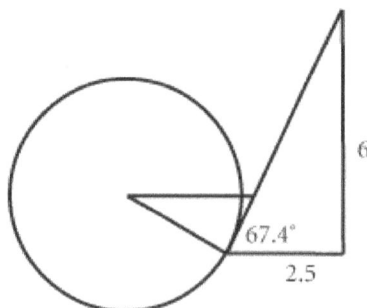

The rider's path is tangent to the Ferris wheel and thus perpendicular to the radius at the point of tangency. Drawing a horizontal radius past the circle to the rider's path creates a triangle similar to the larger triangle, since the path acts as a transversal cutting two parallel (horizontal) lines. Students should explain how this determines the central angle as 22.6°. They might use a variety of proportions to show that this angle corresponds to about 45 clock minutes, so the clock position is 3:45. A totally different approach might involve imagining that you're riding on the Ferris wheel looking straight ahead (in the direction of motion) and thinking how far you've turned (from 3 o'clock) to get to this position.

Question 3 gives students an opportunity to retrace their specific solutions to Questions 2a and 2b and so to describe a general procedure. You might point out that the process of finding the angle becomes more complicated outside the first quadrant (we will not pursue that idea further in this unit).

Key Question

For what angles θ is $\sin^2 \theta + \cos^2 \theta = 1$ a true statement?

Velocities on the Wheel

Intent

Students develop formulas for the horizontal and vertical components of the diver's initial velocity upon release from the Ferris wheel.

Mathematics

This activity requires students to find the relationship between the time that the Ferris wheel has been moving and the horizontal and vertical components of the diver's initial velocity.

Progression

Students work on the activity individually. The follow-up discussion will produce the final key formulas for the central unit problem. Students will confirm in *Release at Any Angle* that these formulas work in all four quadrants.

Approximate Time

20 to 30 minutes for activity (at home or in class)
15 to 20 minutes for discussion

Classroom Organization

Individuals, followed by whole-class discussion

Discussing and Debriefing the Activity

Except for the choice of release position, Question 1 is identical to Questions 1 and 2 of *One O'Clock Without Gravity*. Students should show that the platform has turned through a 72° angle. Thus, the vertical component of velocity is 7.85 cos 72°, so the diver is initially moving upward at approximately 2.43 ft/s. The horizontal component of velocity is −7.85 sin 72°, so the diver is initially moving to the left at approximately 7.47 ft/s.

By comparison, in the discussion of *One O'Clock Without Gravity*, students found the vertical component to be 3.9 ft/s and the horizontal component to be −6.8 ft/s. Ask, **Do the differences between this activity's results and the results in** *One O'Clock Without Gravity* **make sense?** Students should see that the larger angle in *Velocities on the Wheel* means the diver's initial velocity is "more horizontal" and recognize that this is consistent with the results. Sketching vector diagrams may help illustrate the effect.

For Question 2, students should be able to generalize their work from Question 1 and from *One O'Clock Without Gravity* to get the following expressions for the case in which the diver is released within the first quadrant ($0 < W < 10$):

- Vertical component of velocity: $7.85 \cos (9W)$
- Horizontal component of velocity: $-7.85 \sin (9W)$

The expression $9W$ represents the angle of rotation after traveling for W seconds, as used earlier in the unit.

As with the specific examples, be sure students recognize the significance of the minus sign for the horizontal component. They should see that for angles in the first quadrant, the diver's horizontal movement will be to the left, so this component of velocity needs to be negative.

For Question 3a, students should see (from a diagram or similar analysis) that the vertical component of the diver's velocity is positive if the diver is released in either the first or fourth quadrant, which means W is either less than 10 or more than 30. Similarly, the vertical component of the diver's velocity is negative if W is between 10 and 30, and zero for both $W = 10$ and $W = 30$.

For Question 3b, students should see that the horizontal component of the diver's velocity is positive if W is greater than 20, negative if W is less than 20, and zero at 0, 20, and 40.

You may want to post these conclusions, as they will be referred to in the next activity, *Release at Any Angle*.

Key Question

Do the differences between this activity's results and the results in *One O'Clock Without Gravity* make sense?

Release at Any Angle

Intent

Students find general expressions for the vertical and horizontal components of the diver's velocity in the main unit problem.

Mathematics

In *Velocities on the Wheel,* students developed expressions for the vertical and horizontal components of the diver's initial velocity as he is released from a first-quadrant position on the Ferris wheel. Now they test whether those expressions work in all four quadrants.

Progression

Students work on the activity in groups. In the follow-up discussion, the class confirms that the expressions for the vertical and horizontal components of the diver's initial velocity work in all four quadrants.

Approximate Time

30 to 35 minutes

Classroom Organization

Small groups, followed by whole-class discussion

Doing the Activity

In Question 2 of *Velocities on the Wheel,* students developed expressions for the components of the diver's initial velocity. Thus far, they have considered only the case in which the diver is released within the first quadrant—that is, for $0 < W < 10$. Tell them that they will now examine whether these expressions work for all points of release.

Let students work on the activity in groups. The goal of Questions 1b and 1c is to verify that a graph based on the expression is consistent with an intuitive, qualitative analysis of the situation.

Even if groups have not finished the activity, allow a few minutes at the end of class to discuss at least through Question 1c and to assure the class that the expressions do, in fact, work for all values of W.

Discussing and Debriefing the Activity

Have a student sketch a graph based on the proposed equation for the vertical component of velocity (Question 1a). As a class, verify (see Question 1b) that the graph is consistent with the sign analysis from *Velocities on the Wheel.*

For Question 1c, have another student describe, based on the situation, how the vertical component of velocity changes in size as W increases from 10 to 20. The presenter should note that at $W = 10$, the diver's initial motion is horizontal, so the vertical component is zero, and that as W increases, his motion becomes more directly downward so that the size (absolute value) of the vertical component increases (becoming "more negative"). Again, confirm as a class that this is consistent with the graph.

If time allows and you feel students need the discussion, continue with Question 1d and then Question 2. The key in Question 1d is to confirm that the vertical component of velocity does, in fact, increase in absolute value as W increases from 11 to 12.

For instance, for $W = 11$, the angle of turn is 99° (which is $9W$), and students might use a diagram like the one below. If they view this diagram sideways so that the upward line is like the positive direction of the x-axis, then the vertical component of the diver's initial motion is like the x-coordinate of a point on the ray showing that motion. Students have already seen, in discussing the Ferris wheel problem, that they can find a point's x-coordinate by multiplying its r-value by cos θ. Here, the overall speed, 7.85 ft/s, is like that r-value, and the vertical component of the diver's initial motion is 7.85 cos 99°. Bring out that this is negative but not very large (in absolute value), just as cos 99° is negative but not very large.

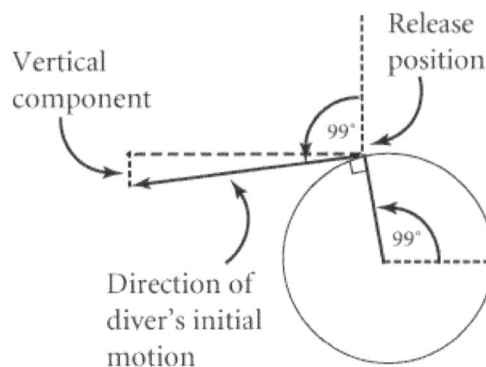

Before concluding, assure students that the formulas do work for all angles, and post the formulas along with the others around the room. To have more precise values available for the final solution of the unit problem, use the exact value of

2.5π ft/s (rather than 7.85 ft/s) as the platform's speed as it turns around on the Ferris wheel.

If the diver is released _W_ seconds after passing the 3 o'clock position, his initial velocity will have these components:
- **Vertical component of velocity: 2.5π cos (9_W_)**
- **Horizontal component of velocity: −2.5π sin (9_W_)**

An Expanded Portfolio of Formulas

Intent

Students summarize the formulas related to the unit problem.

Mathematics

In *A Simple Summary and a Complex Beginning*, students compiled a list of formulas that they used to solve the simplified version of the unit problem. In the discussion following that activity, they speculated how the formulas might need to be changed once the effects of the diver's initial motion due to the turning of the Ferris wheel were considered. Now they return to that list and consider how the formulas need to be adjusted and what additional formulas are necessary.

Progression

Students work individually to compile their lists of formulas. In the subsequent discussion, they share formulas but do not talk about how to use them to solve the unit problem. *An Expanded Portfolio of Formulas* will be part of the unit portfolio.

Approximate Time

30 minutes for activity (at home or in class)
10 to 15 minutes for discussion

Classroom Organization

Individuals, followed by whole-class discussion

Doing the Activity

If assigning this activity as homework, you may want to give students some time to take notes on what's posted around the classroom, including the compilation of formulas from *A Simple Summary and a Complex Beginning.*

Point out to students that this activity will be included in their portfolios for this unit.

Discussing and Debriefing the Activity

Here is the list of the key formulas for the simplified problem as given in the discussion following *A Simple Summary and a Complex Beginning*. (Your class may have a somewhat different list.)

- Diver's height at time of release: $65 + 50 \sin (9W)$

- Diver's horizontal coordinate at time of release: 50 cos (9W)
- Distance the diver falls: 57 + 50 sin (9W)
- Time the diver falls: $\sqrt{\dfrac{57 + 50 \ \sin \ (9W)}{16}}$

- Time the cart travels until the diver reaches the water level:
  $W + \sqrt{\dfrac{57 + 50 \ \sin \ (9W)}{16}}$
- Cart's horizontal coordinate when diver reaches the water level:
  $-240 + 15\left(W + \sqrt{\dfrac{57 + 50 \ \sin \ (9W)}{16}} \right)$

The first three formulas can be used without change, because they relate only to what happens before the diver is released.

The formula for the time for the diver's fall will change in order to take into account the diver's initial vertical velocity. Students might recognize that they need to combine two new ideas to get the new formula:

- The vertical component of the diver's velocity is $2.5\pi \cos (9W)$, as found in *Release at Any Angle*.
- If the vertical component of the diver's velocity is v, then his falling time is $\dfrac{v + \sqrt{v^2 + 64h}}{32}$, as found in the discussion of *Falling Time for Vertical Motion*. A better description for this quantity might be "duration of the dive after release," since the diver may actually be rising for the first portion of the dive. Likewise, the expression 57 + 50 sin (9W) is the vertical distance from the diver's point of release to the water level, but he may actually travel a greater total vertical distance during his dive.

The change in the time of the diver's fall will also affect the last two formulas in the list, requiring that the expression $\sqrt{\dfrac{57 + 50 \ \sin \ (9W)}{16}}$ be replaced by $\dfrac{v + \sqrt{v^2 + 64h}}{32}$, with v replaced by $2.5\pi \cos (9W)$. (Students might identify the quadratic formula as a "new formula" they need, because they used this to develop the falling-time formula.)

Finally, students will need to take into account the horizontal component of the diver's initial velocity. In *Release at Any Angle*, they found that this horizontal component is $-2.5\pi \sin (9W)$.

This horizontal velocity in turn affects the diver's horizontal coordinate when he reaches the water level. In the simplified version of the problem, this was the same as his horizontal coordinate at the time of release. Now, the diver's horizontal coordinate when he reaches the water level depends on his coordinate at the time of release, the horizontal component of his velocity upon release, and the duration of his fall. Students might combine these elements into a single formula or simply give a verbal description of how to combine them.

Moving Diver at Two O'Clock

Intent

Students put together much of what they have learned to analyze a specific situation related to the unit problem.

Mathematics

Students do a complete analysis for a Ferris wheel situation involving both vertical and horizontal initial velocity, finding the diver's falling time and both the diver's and the cart's horizontal positions when the diver reaches the water level.

Progression

Students work in groups to apply the formulas just developed to another Ferris wheel situation. The subsequent discussion provides an opportunity to review the general principles of the unit.

Approximate Time

40 minutes

Classroom Organization

Small groups, followed by whole-class discussion

Doing the Activity

Assure students that they can use all the formulas and principles that have been posted around the classroom, as students are sometimes tempted to develop these formulas again.

You will likely want fairly detailed presentations on Questions 1 and 2. You may want to give groups materials to use for preparing these presentations.

Discussing and Debriefing the Activity

For Question 1, students will probably go through steps like these:
- The diver's height when he is released is $65 + 50 \sin 30° = 90$ feet.
- The vertical component of his initial velocity is $2.5\pi \cdot \cos 30° \approx 6.80$ ft/s.
- The diver's height t seconds after release is given by the expression $90 + 6.80t - 16t^2$.
- The answer to Question 1 is the positive solution to the equation $90 + 6.80t - 16t^2 = 8$. Students will probably put this equation in standard

form as $16t^2 - 6.80t - 82 = 0$ and solve it using the quadratic formula. The solution is given by the expression

$$\frac{6.80 + \sqrt{6.80^2 + 64 \cdot 82}}{32}$$

which gives $t \approx 2.49$ seconds.

Each part of this analysis represents the application of a formula that has been developed at some point in the unit. You may want to identify the relevant posted formula or result as each part is discussed.

For Question 2, the task is a bit simpler, because the falling time (more accurately, the length of time after release) has already been found.
- The diver's x-coordinate when he is released is $50 \cos 30° \approx 43.3$ feet (to the right of center).
- The horizontal component of his initial velocity is $-2.5\pi \cdot \sin 30° \approx -3.93$ ft/s, which means he is moving to the left.
- The diver takes 2.49 seconds to fall to the water level.
- The diver moves about $2.49 \cdot (-3.93) \approx -9.8$ feet while falling, so his position when he reaches the water level is about $43.3 - 9.8 = 33.5$, or about 33.5 feet to the right of center.

The analysis for Question 3 will probably go something like this:
- The diver is on the Ferris wheel for $30 \div 9 \approx 3.33$ seconds before being released.
- The diver takes 2.49 seconds to fall to the water level.
- Altogether, the cart is moving for $3.33 + 2.49 = 5.82$ seconds.
- The cart starts 240 feet to the left of center, so its initial position is –240.
- The cart travels 15 ft/s, so it travels a total of about $5.82 \cdot 15 = 87.3$ feet to the right.
- The cart's position when the diver reaches the water level is $-240 + 87.3 = -152.7$, so the cart is 152.7 feet to the left of center.

Have students summarize what would happen if this scenario actually took place. The diver would land about 33.5 feet to the right of center, while the cart would be 152.7 feet to the left of center, so the cart would miss the diver by 186.2 feet.

The Danger of Simplification

Intent

Students examine the effect of the diver's initial velocity using the value of W that worked for the simplified unit problem.

Mathematics

Now students consider what will happen to the diver if they use the result from *Moving Cart, Turning Ferris Wheel* but take into account the diver's initial velocity due to the motion of the Ferris wheel.

Progression

Students work on the activity individually or in groups. The subsequent discussion emphasizes that the diver's initial velocity has a significant effect on the result.

Approximate Time

25 minutes for activity (at home or in class)
20 minutes for discussion

Classroom Organization

Individuals or small groups, followed by whole-class discussion

Doing the Activity

Students can begin on the activity with no introduction. Note that although they may have found a more precise answer, such as 12.28 seconds, for *Moving Cart, Turning Ferris Wheel,* the difference between that value and the value of 12.3 seconds used here does not have a significant impact on the outcome. The "performance error" that emerges in the latter analysis is virtually all due to the diver's initial velocity.

Discussing and Debriefing the Activity

The main task in this activity is finding the answer to Question 1. The analysis is given in some detail here for your reference. Students will need to generalize this process to solve the unit problem, however, so they need to develop the ideas themselves.

Question 1

To answer Question 1, students first need to find the diver's height upon release and the vertical component of his initial velocity. (We also present here his horizontal position upon release and the horizontal component of his initial velocity. Students do not need these values until Question 2, but are likely to find them as part of this preliminary stage of the analysis.)

Although students have formulas for these components, this may be the first time they have used them for a non-first-quadrant case, so you may want to discuss the details. Students should reach these conclusions for $W = 12.3$:

- The vertical velocity component is given by the expression

  $2.5\pi \cos (9 \cdot 12.3)$, which yields a value of approximately –2.78 ft/s. This is consistent with the fact that in the second quadrant, the diver is moving downward.
- The horizontal velocity component is given by the expression

  $-2.5\pi \sin (9 \cdot 12.3)$, which yields a value of approximately –7.35 ft/s. This is consistent with the fact that in the second quadrant, the diver is moving to the left.

You may want to bring out that the horizontal component is larger in magnitude than the vertical component, which reflects the fact that for $W = 12.3$, the diver is on the way from the 12 o'clock to the 11 o'clock position, so his movement is primarily horizontal.

Students also need to determine the diver's position at the moment of release.

- His height above the center of the Ferris wheel is given by the expression

  $50 \sin (9 \cdot 12.3)$, which yields a value of approximately 46.8 feet. This means he is $46.8 + 57 = 103.8$ feet above the water level.
- His x-coordinate (relative to the center of the wheel) is given by the

  expression $50 \cos (9 \cdot 12.3)$, which yields a value of approximately –17.7. This means he is about 17.7 feet to the left of center.

Next, students need to use these results to find the time for the diver to fall to the water level. They might explicitly write down the expression for his height t seconds after release, $103.8 - 2.78t - 16t^2$, and use the quadratic formula to solve the equation obtained by setting this expression equal to 0. Or they might apply the equation for falling time found in *Falling Time for Vertical Motion*:

$$t = \frac{v + \sqrt{v^2 + 64h}}{32}$$

where v is the vertical component of velocity (–2.78 ft/s, in this case) and h is the distance the diver falls (103.8 feet).

In either case, students should reach this conclusion for Question 1: If the diver is released after 12.3 seconds, he will reach the water level in approximately 2.46 seconds.

Now might be a good time to introduce the variable F to distinguish the falling time from W, the length of time on the Ferris wheel, giving $W = 12.3$ seconds and $F = 2.46$ seconds.

Questions 2 and 3

Once the falling time is determined, the remaining analysis is fairly straightforward. After release, the diver moves to the left at 7.35 ft/s for 2.46 seconds, starting at $x = -17.7$, so his x-coordinate when he reaches the water level can be found from the expression

$$-17.7 + 2.46 \cdot (-7.35)$$

This comes out to approximately −35.8. That is, the diver reaches the water level approximately 35.8 feet to the left of the Ferris wheel's center.

For Question 3, the cart moves to the right at 15 ft/s both while the diver is on the Ferris wheel (12.3 seconds) and while he is falling (2.46 seconds). The cart starts at $x = -240$, so its x-coordinate at the time the diver reaches the water level is found from the expression

$$-240 + (12.3 + 2.46) \cdot 15$$

This comes out to approximately −18.6, so at the moment the diver reaches the water level, the cart is approximately 18.6 feet to the left of the Ferris wheel's center.

Question 4

You may want to play up the drama of the conclusion from Question 4. Students should have discovered that the diver misses the cart by approximately 17.2 feet! This demonstrates the significance of the work students have been doing in considering the diver's initial velocity. (Of course, the dimensions of the tub are never specified. Perhaps the tub is wide enough to deal with this level of miscalculation.)

Looking Back

You may want to compare these results with those from *Moving Cart, Turning Ferris Wheel.* In that simplified version of the problem, the diver's x-coordinate throughout his fall was −17.5, and his falling time was about 2.55 seconds.

The vertical component of the diver's initial velocity shortened his falling time slightly (from 2.55 seconds to 2.46 seconds), which means the cart is not as far along the track. (It's at −18.6 instead of −17.5.) But the horizontal component of the diver's initial velocity had a substantial effect. He ends up at $x = -35.8$, instead of at $x = -17.5$, more than 18 feet farther to the left. Ouch!

The Diver Really Returns

Intent

In these activities, students solve the unit problem.

Mathematics

These activities relate to solving the unit problem and wrapping up the unit.

Progression

Students solve the unit problem in the culminating activity, *The Diver's Success*. The unit concludes with reflections and unit portfolios.

The Diver's Success
A Circus Reflection
Beginning Portfolio Selection
"The Diver Returns" Portfolio

The Diver's Success

Intent

Students solve the unit problem.

Mathematics

Students now have knowledge of all the concepts necessary to solve the unit problem. Their first task will be to synthesize what they have learned in order to formulate an equation that represents the problem situation. The more formidable task may be to enter this complex equation into a calculator and solve it—probably graphically, as the equation defies solution by way of algebraic manipulation.

Progression

Students will work in groups on this activity. They will likely need some assistance, particularly in remembering the mechanics of how to split a large function into several manageable pieces in the calculator.

Approximate Time

65 minutes

Classroom Organization

Small groups, followed by whole-class discussion

Doing the Activity

Have students work in groups, but ask that they complete individual reports. You may want to offer assistance as groups proceed, especially about how to define some functions in terms of others to avoid excessively complex expressions on the calculator.

Discussing and Debriefing the Activity

You may wish to have different groups present various parts of the solution to maintain interest in the process. You might have a group that did not finish the problem present first, and then have other groups follow up to describe how they continued from that point.

If students did not get the correct answer, you might let them rework their reports for homework. Students may want to use their reports in studying for the assessment or preparing their portfolios. The report should be included in everyone's portfolio.

An Outline of the Solution

The following possible approach to solving the problem is a synthesis of ideas developed over the course of the unit.

As indicated in the activity, $t = 0$ represents the time when the cart begins moving and $t = W$ represents the time at which the diver is released. These variables represent other components of the solution:

- *h:* the diver's height above the water level at the time of release
$$h = 57 + 50 \sin (9W)$$
- *c:* the diver's *x*-coordinate at the time of release
$$c = 50 \cos (9W)$$
- v_y: the vertical component of the diver's velocity when he is released
$$v_y = 2.5\pi \cos (9W)$$
- v_x: the horizontal component of the diver's velocity when he is released
$$v_x = - 2.5\pi \sin (9W)$$
- *F:* the duration of the diver's fall from the time of release until he reaches the water level

$$F = \frac{v_y + \sqrt{v_y^{\,2} + 64h}}{32}$$

This expression comes from using the expression $h + v_y t - 16t^2$ for the diver's height above the water level t seconds after he is released and solving the equation $h + v_y t - 16t^2 = 0$. In standard form, this equation is $16t^2 - v_y t - h = 0$, so for the purposes of the quadratic formula, $a = 16$, $b = -v_y$, and $c = -h$. In applying the quadratic formula in this context, we want the "+" portion of the ± sign.

Based on these variables, students can find expressions for other aspects of the problem:

- $W + F$: the total time the cart is moving
- $-240 + 15(W + F)$: the *x*-coordinate of the cart at the time the diver reaches the water level
- $c + v_x F$: the *x*-coordinate of the diver when he reaches the water level

The task is to find the value of W that puts the cart in the right place at the right time. Based on the two expressions just given for the positions of the cart and the diver at the time the diver reaches the water level, we need to find the value of W that solves the equation

$$-240 + 15(W + F) = c + v_xF$$

It turns out that the desired value is $W \approx 11.45$ seconds. If the diver is released 11.45 seconds after the cart starts, he lands in the water about 30.54 feet to the left of the Ferris wheel's base (or 30.53 feet if you use the unrounded value of W).

You may want to ask students to trace this value of W through the problem.

For your convenience, here are the values of the different pieces of the puzzle. These results were found using a more precise value for W of 11.449 seconds. Final values were rounded to the nearest hundredth, but values for expressions such as $W + F$, $c + v_xF$, and $-240 + 15(W + F)$ were initially found using pre-round-off values for the variables in those expressions.

- $h = 105.71$ (The diver is 105.71 feet above the water level when released.)
- $c = -11.28$ (The diver is 11.28 feet to the left of center when released.)
- $v_y = -1.77$ (The diver has an initial vertical component of velocity of 1.77 ft/sec downward.)
- $v_x = -7.65$ (The diver has an initial horizontal component of velocity of 7.65 ft/sec to the left.)
- $F = 2.52$ (The diver is in the air for 2.52 seconds.)
- $W + F = 13.96$ (The cart travels for 13.96 seconds.)
- $c + v_xF = -30.54$ (The diver is 30.54 feet to the left of center when he reaches the water level.)
- $-240 + 15(W + F) = -30.54$ (The cart is 30.54 feet to the left of center when the diver reaches the water level.)

You may want to have students compare this result with the analyses they did in *Moving Cart, Turning Ferris Wheel* and *The Danger of Simplification*.

Finally, you might want to point out that we have ignored a whole separate problem, which is more a question of physiology than mathematics or physics: Could the diver survive the dive into the water?

Key Question

Could the diver survive the dive into the water?

A Circus Reflection

Intent

Students consider situations in which oversimplification might lead to serious consequences.

Mathematics

Simplifying assumptions are often valuable and necessary tools for modeling a real-life situation mathematically. However, as students just saw in *The Danger of Simplification*, an oversimplification can lead to a solution that is not realistic or useful.

Progression

Students answer the questions on their own and share ideas in a class discussion.

Approximate Time

15 minutes for activity (at home or in class)
10 minutes for discussion

Classroom Organization

Individuals, followed by whole-class discussion

Doing the Activity

This activity requires no introduction.

Discussing and Debriefing the Activity

Have students share some of the scenarios they imagined in Question 2.

Beginning Portfolio Selection

Intent

Students begin to select material for the unit portfolio.

Mathematics

The focus of the activity is on the connections among quadratic equations, complex numbers, and vectors.

Progression

Students select activities that helped them see connections among major topics in the unit and then share their ideas in class.

Approximate Time

30 minutes for activity (at home or in class)

Classroom Organization

Individuals

Doing the Activity

This activity requires no introduction.

Discussing and Debriefing the Activity

You might have students discuss their selections and reflections in small groups. You may also want to have a couple of volunteers share which activities they chose and the connections they made.

"The Diver Returns" Portfolio

Intent

Students reflect upon the key concepts of the unit as they compile their unit portfolios and write their cover letters.

Mathematics

As students pull together all the information they have studied in the unit, they consider how it all fits together to develop the unit's main ideas and to solve the unit problem.

Progression

Students complete their unit portfolios, selecting key activities and writing their cover letters.

Approximate Time

5 minutes for introduction
30 to 40 minutes for activity (at home or in class)

Classroom Organization

Individuals

Doing the Activity

Have students read the instructions in the student book carefully.

Discussing and Debriefing the Activity

You may want to have a few volunteers read their cover letters to start a discussion summarizing the key ideas of the unit.

Blackline Masters

The Circus Act

As the Ferris Wheel Turns

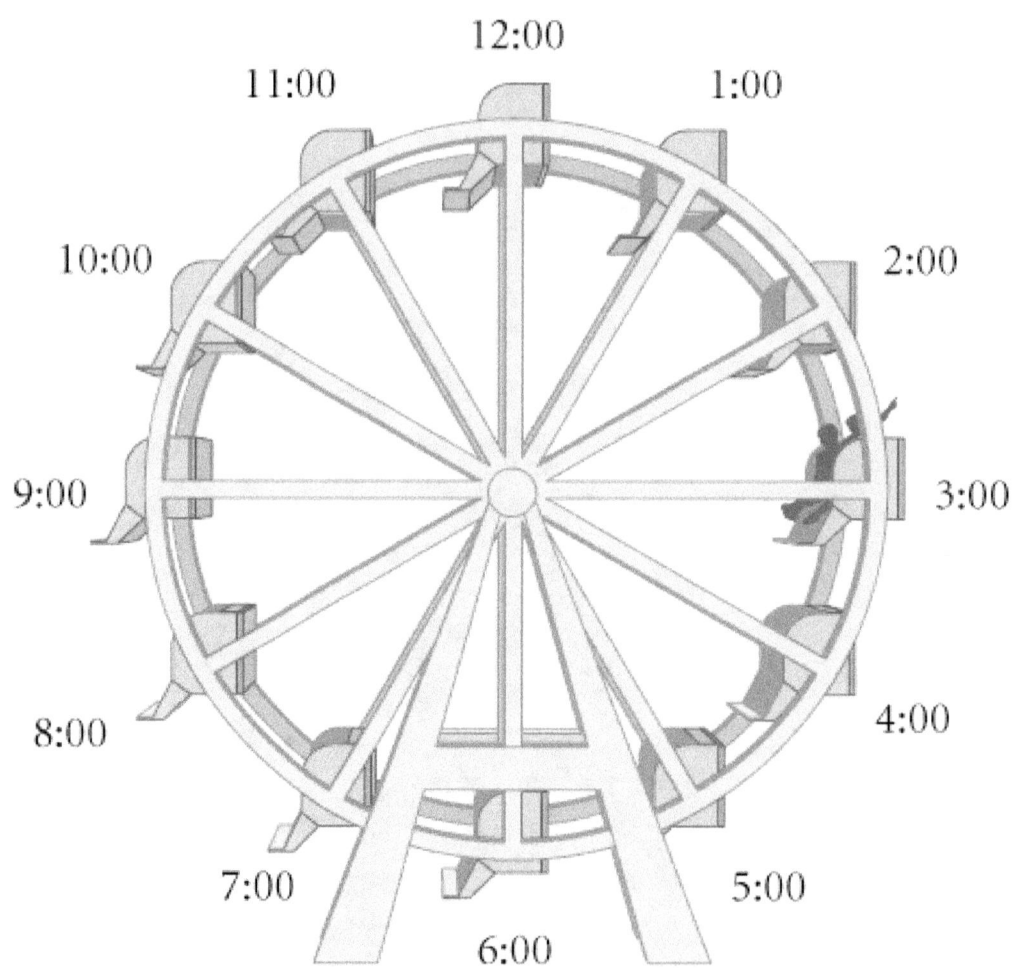

12:00
11:00   1:00
10:00   2:00
9:00   3:00
8:00   4:00
7:00   5:00
6:00

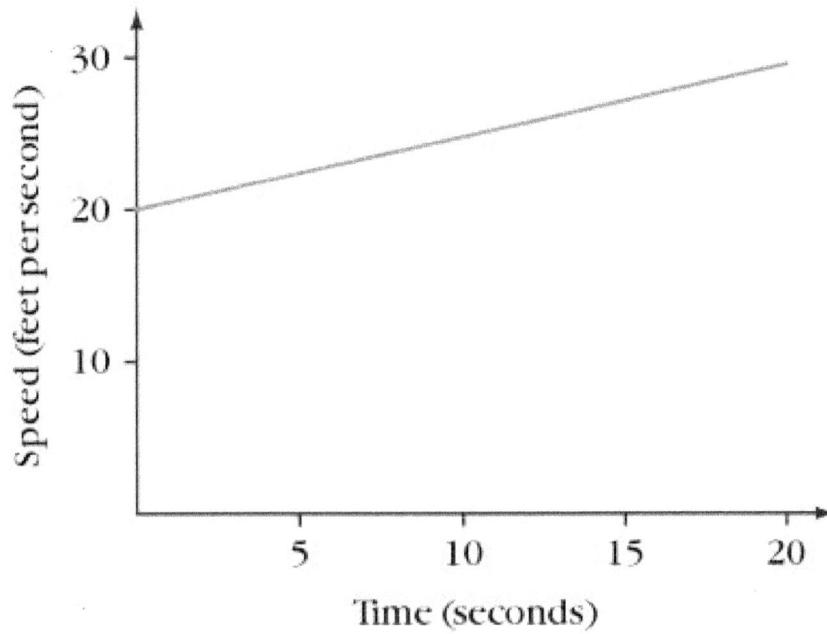

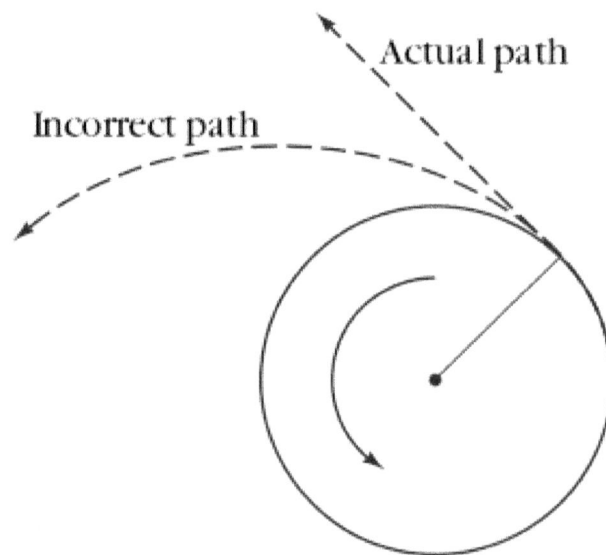

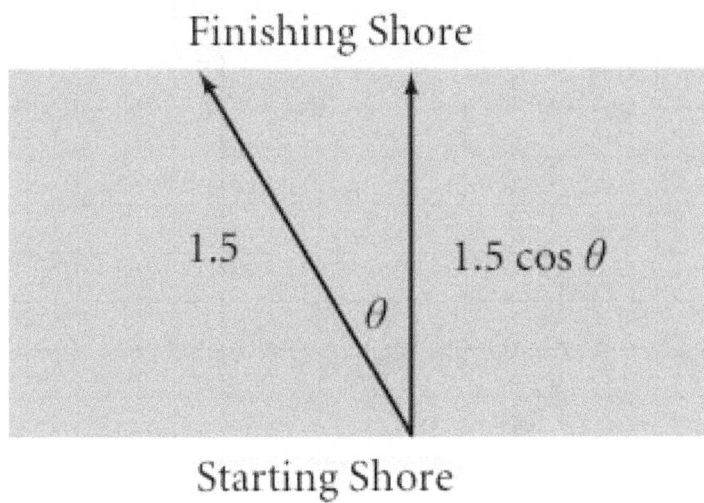

¼-Inch Graph Paper

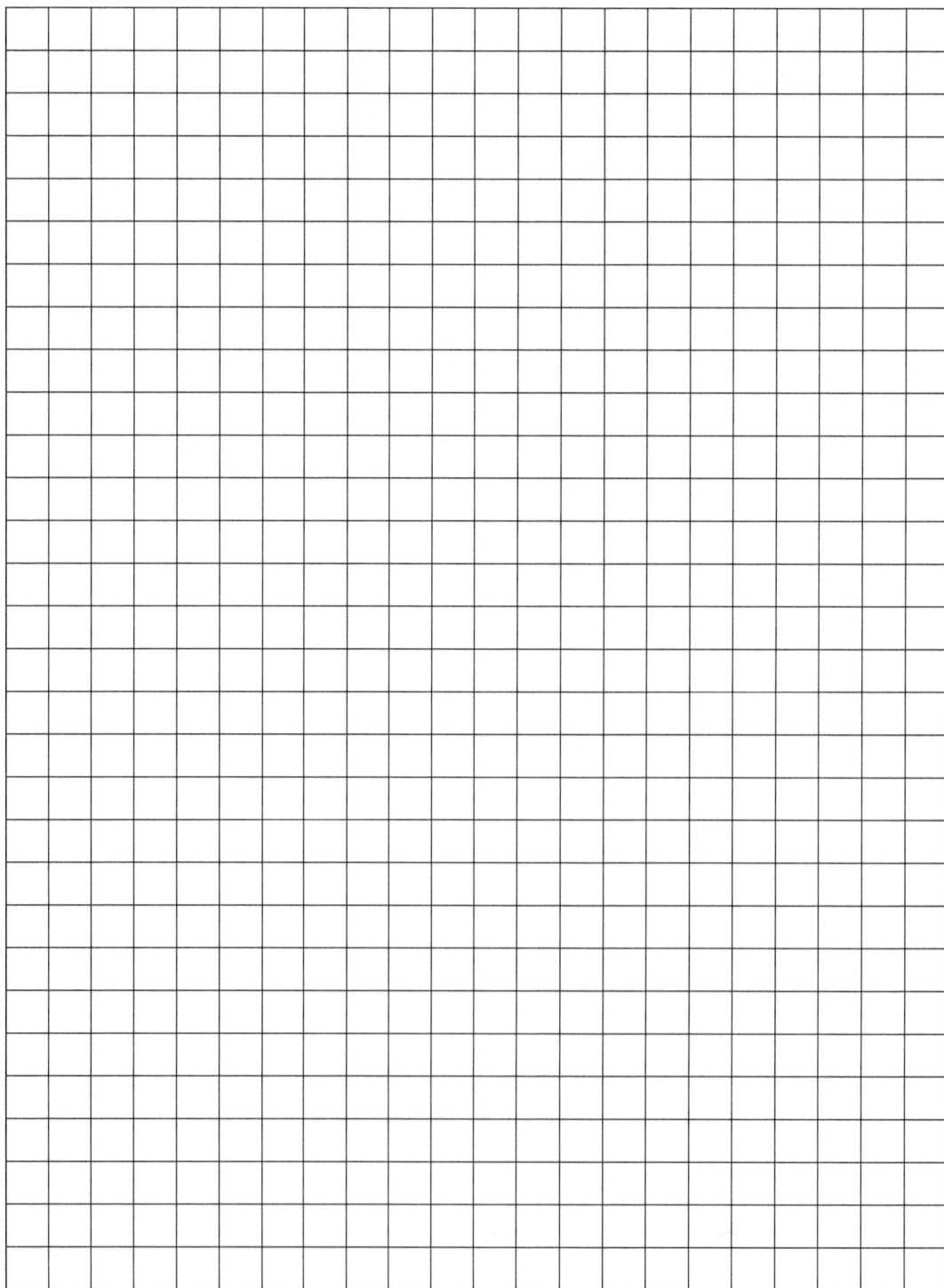

1-Centimeter Graph Paper

1-Inch Graph Paper

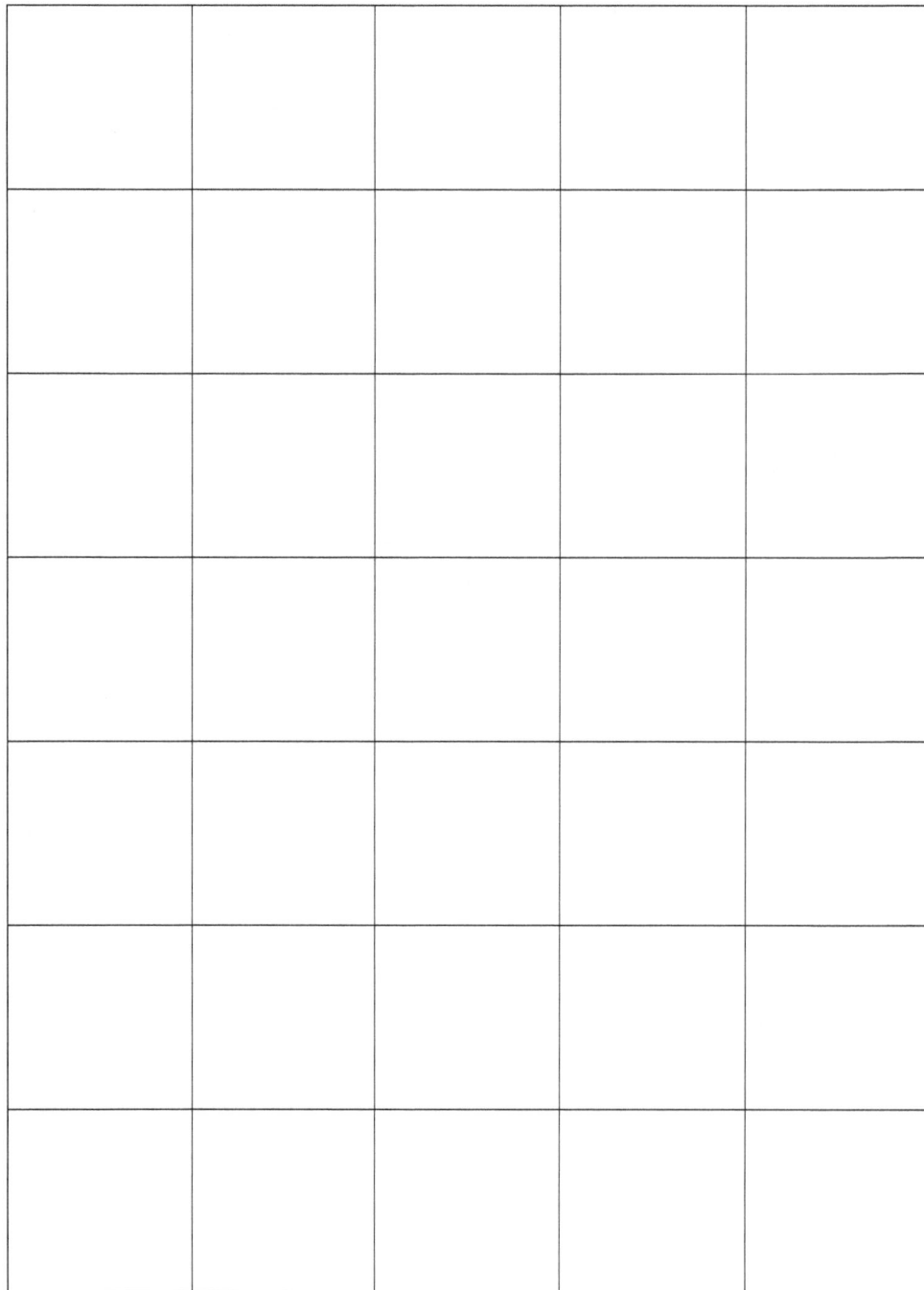

Assessments

In-Class Assessment

1. Solve the quadratic equation $x^2 + 4x - 3 = 0$ in each of these two ways.

    a. By completing the square

    b. By using the quadratic formula

    Show your work in each case. Give your answers in two ways: (1) in exact form using square roots and (2) to the nearest tenth.

2. Sketch a graph of the function $y = x^2 + 4x - 3$, using information from Question 1. Explain how you used that information.

3. a. Show by substitution that both $4 + 3i$ and $4 - 3i$ are solutions to the equation $x^2 - 8x + 25 = 0$.

    b. Explain what this tells you about the graph of the function $y = x^2 - 8x + 25$.

Take-Home Assessment

Sabrina does a swing act in the circus. At the end of her act, she gets the swing going really fast. As she is on the upward part of her swing forward, she lets go and flies up and forward from the swing.

At the moment she lets go, she is moving at 30 feet per second, she is 11 feet off the ground, and the swing is at an angle of 30° from vertical. She will land on a foam pad that is 1 foot thick.

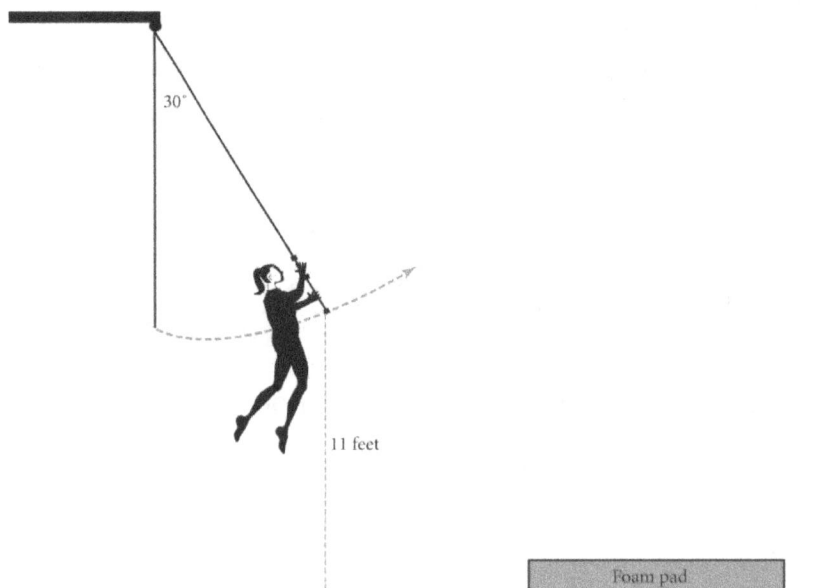

Assume that Sabrina's path after she lets go is based only on her initial velocity and the usual gravitational acceleration rate, with no air resistance or other complications.

1. From the moment Sabrina lets go, how long will it take until she hits the foam pad?

2. How far forward will Sabrina fly from the point where she leaves the swing until she hits the pad?

3. How fast will she be going when she hits the pad?

Give your answers to the nearest tenth of a second, the nearest tenth of a foot per second, or the nearest tenth of a foot, as appropriate.

I. The Diver Returns

1. Mike plays the tuba. His college's marching band is performing at halftime. At one point in the performance, the band members form a 100-foot-diameter circle in the center of the field. As the band begins to march around the circle, Mike is at the end of the circle closest to the goal line, which is 100 feet away. How far from the same goal line will he be after he has marched 320 degrees around the circle?

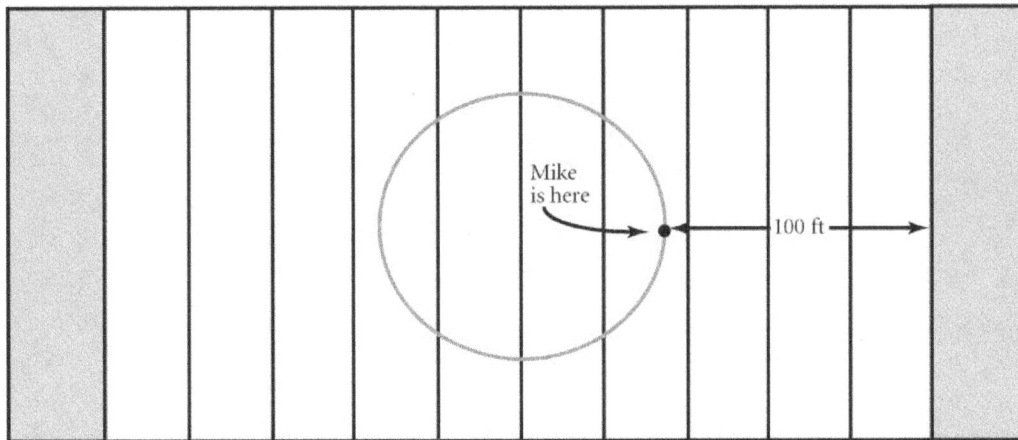

2. A coin is thrown downward with an initial velocity of 5 feet per second at an angle of $37°$ below the horizontal.

   a. How far will the coin move horizontally in the first 3 seconds?

   b. How far will the coin fall vertically in the first 3 seconds?

II. The World of Functions

1. a. Sketch the graph of a function that has both of these properties:

   - As *x* becomes very large in the positive direction, *y* becomes very large in the positive direction.
   - As *x* becomes very large in the negative direction, the graph has the *x*-axis as an asymptote.

   b. What is a possible algebraic equation that describes a graph like this? Explain.

2. The table shows the outputs for a function *f* for a given set of input values.

x	f(x)
−3	3
−2	0
−1	−1
0	0
1	3
2	8
3	15

   a. Plot the points represented by this table.

   b. Decide what family you think the function belongs to, and explain your reasoning.

   c. Find an algebraic expression for *f* that fits the information in the table.

III. The Pollster's Dilemma

1. You are one of two candidates running for office. Eighty percent of the population plans to vote for you. Of course, being humble, you have no idea that 0.8 is the true proportion. Though everyone keeps telling you that you will win, you don't quite believe it.

   When a 7-person poll is conducted, you say that you will eat your hat if five or more of the respondents plan to vote for you. What is the probability that you will be glad you have a very small hat size—that is, that five or more will say they plan to vote for you?

2. A driver's license test has a mean score of 63 with a standard deviation of 15. If 75 is the minimal passing score, about what percentage of people who take the test will pass?

The Diver Returns Calculator Guide for the TI-83/84 Family of Calculators

The Diver Returns is an extension of the Year 3 unit *High Dive,* and will benefit from the continued use of several of the graphing calculator techniques learned then.

The unit problem itself leads to an equation that is far too complex to solve by algebraic manipulations and that instead is solved graphically with the calculator. Even a graphical solution without the calculator would be awkward. Students should gain a tremendous sense of satisfaction at having solved an impossible-looking equation, as well as an appreciation for the power of the graphing calculator.

Throughout the unit, students can use the calculator to check graphically what they discover with algebra and trigonometry. The second week provides an appropriate context in which to reveal the CALC menu full of helpful features. As students begin, near the end of the unit, to pull together the many elements of the unit problem, they will learn how to break lengthy functions into smaller pieces for entry into the calculator. After the unit problem has been solved, a parametric demonstration on the calculator can provide both a vivid illustration of their solution and an introduction to parametric equations, which they may explore further in the *Know How* unit.

As noted previously, students who are new to IMP will be at a disadvantage if they have not worked extensively with a graphing calculator. You may need to provide these students with access to calculators and instruction outside of class time.

Finding with the Formula: As students begin work on evaluating the quadratic formula, they will need to be careful in three areas relative to their use of the calculator.

First, if $b = -3$, for example, they need to realize that b^2 is not equal to -3^2. As shown here, the calculator correctly performs exponentiation before negation and interprets -3^2 as $-(3^2)$. Encourage students to perform substitution by replacing the variable with an empty set of parentheses and then "dropping" the value of the variable into the parentheses.

```
-3²
            -9
(-3)²
            9
```

If students choose to enter large sections of the formula at a time, they need to be very careful with parentheses. When evaluating $\sqrt{b^2 - 4ac}$, calculator users must close the parentheses that the calculator opens.

When dividing by 2*a*, students need to place parentheses around the denominator of the formula. For example, if the formula has been simplified to $\dfrac{24}{3 \bullet 2}$, a brief review of the order of operations will confirm that entering **24/3*2** will not give the correct result.

```
24/3*2
              16
24/(3*2)
               4
```

If students enter the entire formula at once, they also need to use parentheses around the entire numerator. Even then, it is easy to forget to close both sets of parentheses—those around the numerator and those around the radicand—before moving on to the denominator.

If you have time, let students talk you through the process of generating a simple calculator program for evaluating the quadratic formula. Then have them enter either the programs they have generated or the program given in the Calculator Note "Programming the Quadratic Formula." Basic programming instructions are also provided in the Calculator Note *"Entering a Program into the Calculator,"* and can be used before students enter either their own program or the one provided. Have them save these instructions for use in the unit *As the Cube Turns*.

At first, it might not seem like a good idea for students to have a program for evaluating the quadratic formula at this point. However, as long as you continue to require them to show their work for each problem, there are actually several benefits from doing so. First, it is a wonderful demonstration of the power of the quadratic formula compared to factoring or completing the square, one that lends itself to programming and works with numbers that may not be "friendly." Second, the simplicity of the program, combined with the powerful result, often ignites students' interest in programming. It is eye opening to discover that one can write and enter a program that will evaluate the formula in a fraction of a second, in about the same amount of time it takes to evaluate the formula once by hand. Finally, students who have the program available to check their work actually tend to get more practice with the formula while doing their assignments, not less. As long as they are still required to show their work, the program merely gives them a way to check their answers. When their answers are wrong, the program makes them aware that there is an error in their work, and they usually spend more time locating the error, instead of simply quitting.

The general outline of the program should look something like this:

- Enter the coefficients *a, b,* and *c,* and assign them to variables.
- Evaluate the radical expression.

- Evaluate the entire formula, using a + sign in front of the radical expression.

- Evaluate the entire formula again, using a − sign in front of the radical expression.

- Display the answers.

The program presented in the Calculator Note will give an error message and stop if it encounters a negative value for the radicand. After students learn more about complex numbers later in this unit, and about programming in the unit *As the Cube Turns,* you may want to suggest that they modify the program to handle that situation more gracefully. In the meantime, it is better to leave the program simple, impressing students with the relative ease of adapting the quadratic formula to a calculator program.

Release at Any Angle: The TABLE feature of the calculator, used in *High Dive,* will again be useful for obtaining the data items to be graphed in *Release at Any Angle*. If your students need review of this feature, see the *High Dive* Calculator Note "Creating Tables on the Calculator."

The Diver's Success: The function-graphing techniques learned in *High Dive* will be useful in this activity. If students need review, see the *High Dive* Calculator Note "Graphing a Complicated Function"

The screens shown here illustrate one possible arrangement of the equations to solve the unit problem. The functions are arranged in the same order in which they are presented in the Discussion section of *The Diver's Success* in the *Teacher's Guide*. Using the notation from that discussion, we have these functions:

$$Y_1 = h$$

$$Y_2 = c$$

$$Y_3 = v_y$$

$$Y_4 = v_x$$

$$Y_5 = F$$

$$Y_6 = -240 + 15(W + F)$$

$$Y_7 = c + v_x F$$

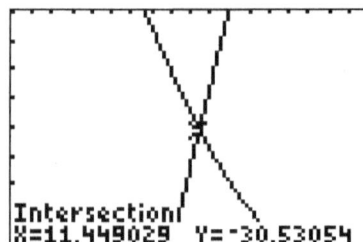

As your class summarizes the unit, you may wish to demonstrate the situation using the following calculator program, which uses parametric equations to show in "real time" what happens with various release times.

There's no need for students to enter this program or even to fully understand how the program works. You might briefly introduce the concept of parametric equations and let students see the equations. Basically, the position of a moving object is broken down into two functions, the *x*-coordinate as a function of time and the *y*-coordinate as a function of time.

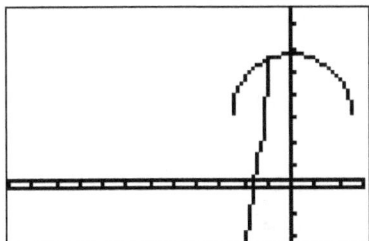

In the program, Function 1 represents the platform's position, Function 2 represents the cart's position, Function 3 represents the diver's position as if falling at that moment, and Function 4 represents the diver's position as either on the platform or falling, depending on the release time.

To start, press PRGM, use the right arrow to select **NEW**, press ENTER to select **Create New**, and enter the name of your program. We suggest **HIGHDIVE** as a name. If students need help with the basics of program entry, have them review the instructions in the Calculator Note "Entering a Program into the Calculator."

Press ENTER after your program name and enter these commands. Of course, you can always simply download the program onto your computer and then onto your calculator, using the instructions found in the Calculator Notes "Linking the Calculator in *Year 4 Calculator Basics.*

Instruction	Explanation
:Degree	Sets the calculator to degree mode. Press MODE, highlight **Degree**, and press ENTER. This inserts the **Degree** command into your program. Press ENTER again to advance to the next program line.
:Param	Sets the calculator to parametric mode. Select **Par** from the MODE screen as described previously.

:Simul

Tells the calculator to graph all functions simultaneously, rather than sequentially. Select **Simul** from the MODE screen.

:Input "DROP TIME?",D

Prompts the user to enter the time at which the diver is dropped (in seconds) and stores this drop time as variable *D*. To find **Input**, press PRGM and use the right arrow to move to the **I/O** menu. Press ENTER to select **1:Input**. The space between **DROP** and **TIME** is an ALPHA character located above the 0 key. If you use [A-LOCK], press ALPHA to shift back out of the ALPHA mode in order to enter the comma near the end of the line.

:Input "SPEED .1 TO .5?",Tstep

Prompts the user to select the speed at which the graph will be drawn, and assigns this value to the variable **Tstep**. (This will be the time increment at which the functions are evaluated and graphed.) To enter **Tstep**, press VARS. From the menu, press ENTER to select **1:Window**. Use the right arrow to highlight **T/θ** and then press 3 to select **3:Tstep**.

:0→Tmin

Sets the lower time limit for which the graph will be drawn. The → represents the STO> key. To find **Tmin**, press VARS ENTER >, similar to **Tstep**.

:20→Tmax

Sets the upper time limit for which the graph will be drawn. To find **Tmax,** start by pressing the VARS key, as described previously.

:-240→Xmin

This group of commands set the window range and axes scale for the graph. Be sure to use the (-) key for the negative sign. **Xmin** and the related variables that follow are found under the **Window** menu after pressing VARS.

:60→Xmax

:20→Xscl

:-10→Ymin

:120→Ymax

:20→Yscl

FnOff

Turns all functions off to keep them from graphing prematurely when the **ZSquare** command is selected in the next line. To find **FnOff**, press VARS, use the right arrow to select **Y-VARS**, and then press 4 followed by 2.

:ZSquare

Adjusts the window range to ensure that the circle of the Ferris wheel will not be distorted. Press ZOOM 5.

:**"50cos(9T)"→X₁ₜ**   Specifies the *x*-coordinate of the platform. Notice that the left side of the command must be enclosed in quotation marks. Use ALPHA [T] to enter the **T**. To enter **X₁ₜ**, press VARS and then use the right arrow to select **Y-VARS**. Then select **2:Parametric** and select the variable from the resulting menu.

:**"65+50sin(9T)"→Y₁ₜ**   Specifies the *y*-coordinate of the platform.

:**"-240+15T"→X₂ₜ**   Specifies the *x*-coordinate of the cart.

:**"8"→Y₂ₜ**   Specifies the *y*-coordinate of the cart.

:**"50cos(9D)-(2.5πsin(9D))*(T-D)" →X₃ₜ**   Specifies the *x*-coordinate of the diver as if falling.

:**"65+50sin(9D)+(2.5πcos(9D))*(T-D)-16(T-D)2"→Y₃ₜ**   Specifies the *y*-coordinate of the diver as if falling. Use the x^2 key for the exponent.

:**"X1T*(T<D)+X3T*(T≥D)"→X₄ₜ**   Specifies the *x*-coordinate of the diver. The two tests (in parentheses) return a value of 1 if true and 0 if false. Thus, if $T < D$, **X₄ₜ** is set equal to **X₁ₜ**. If not, it is set equal to **X₃ₜ**. Do not omit the multiplication symbols in this line. Implied multiplication (such as **X₁ₜ(T<D)**) will not work in this case. To find the inequality symbols, press 2ND [TEST] and then select the appropriate symbol.

:**"Y1T*(T<D)+Y3T*(T≥D)"→Y₄ₜ** Specifies the *y*-coordinate of the diver.

:**FnOff 3**   Turns off graphical display of Function 3, so that Function 4 controls the display of the diver's position.

:**DispGraph**   Displays the graph. Press PRGM, use the right arrow to display the **I/O** menu, and then select **4:DispGraph**.

Press 2ND [QUIT] to exit the editing mode. To run your program, press PRGM and select your program under the **EXEC** menu by highlighting the program name and pressing ENTER. When the program name appears on the home screen, press ENTER again.

When prompted, enter the desired time at which the diver is to be released (in seconds). The next prompt asks you to enter a value between 0.1 and 0.5, which will control the speed at which the graph is drawn. Larger numbers will yield faster animation, but smaller numbers will make it easier to see if the diver and the cart arrive at the same moment.

```
prgmHIGHDIVE
DROP TIME?10
SPEED .1 TO .5?
```

After running the program, press Y= to display the parametric equations and lead a brief discussion of how parametric equations work. When you are finished, you may want to press MODE and return the calculator to the function and sequential modes.

Entering a Program into the Calculator

Starting the Program

If you press the PRGM key, you will see three menu headings across the top of the screen: **EXEC**, from which to execute (run) a program; **EDIT**, from which to edit (change) an existing program; and **NEW**, from which to begin entering a new program.

```
EXEC EDIT NEW
```

To start a new program, press PRGM, use the right arrow to highlight the **NEW** menu heading, and press ENTER to select **Create New**. Notice that the cursor is now a flashing **A**. This means that the calculator is locked in ALPHA mode. Enter a program name of eight characters or less and press ENTER.

```
PROGRAM
Name=█
```

Entering a Program

Every program consists of a series of commands that the calculator executes in order. The calculator marks the beginning of each command with a colon, which the calculator inserts when you press ENTER at the end of the previous line. You can also enter several commands on a single line by separating them with colons.

```
PROGRAM:CHISQUAR
:ClrHome
:Disp "CELL 1 OB
SERVED"
:Input A
:Disp "CELL 2 OB
SERVED"
:Input B
```

You enter most commands into your program by selecting them from menus that are displayed when you press various keys. You cannot enter these commands by spelling them out in ALPHA mode.

Occasionally, you will accidentally select the wrong menu when looking for a program command to insert into your program. When that happens, press CLEAR to return to your program editing. (If you press 2ND [QUIT], the calculator will exit the program editing mode altogether. You will then have to once again select your partially completed program for editing, as described at the end of these instructions.)

Using Input/Output Commands

From within a new program, press the PRGM key and use the right arrow to highlight the **I/O** menu heading. (This will only work if your cursor is within a program. The PRGM key causes a different menu to be displayed when you are editing a program than when you are at the home screen.)

```
CTL I/O EXEC
1:Input
2:Prompt
3:Disp
4:DispGraph
5:DispTable
6:Output(
7↓getKey
```

The **Input** command causes the program to display a question mark and then to pause until the user enters a value. **Input** is followed on the same line by the name of the variable to which the value is to be saved, as shown here.

```
PROGRAM:QUADFORM
:Input A
```

The **Disp** (display) command is followed by the number, variable, expression, or string of text that is to be displayed. Text to be displayed must be enclosed in quotation marks.

```
PROGRAM:PRIME
:Disp N
:Disp "PRESS ENT
ER"
:
:
:
:
:
```

Running a Program

When you finish entering a program, exit the program editing mode by pressing 2ND [QUIT].

Select a program to run by pressing PRGM, highlighting the name of the program in the **EXEC** menu, and then pressing ENTER. The program name will appear on the home screen. Press ENTER again to run the program. If you need to interrupt your program while it is running, press 2ND [QUIT].

```
EXEC EDIT NEW
1:CHISQUAR
2:PRIME
3:QUADFORM
```

Editing a Program

Don't be surprised if your program does not operate as intended the first time. It is usually necessary to return to the program editing mode to revise a new program. These glitches in the program are know as "bugs," and the process of correcting them as "debugging."

To edit your program, press PRGM, highlight the **EDIT** menu heading, highlight the name of your program, and press ENTER.

Programming the Quadratic Formula

These instructions explain how to write a program to evaluate the quadratic formula,

$$x = \frac{-b \pm \sqrt{b^2 - 4ac}}{2a}$$

Begin by giving your program a name. Press PRGM, use the right arrow to highlight **NEW**, and press ENTER. Enter a name of no more than eight letters and press ENTER again. See the Calculator Note "Entering a Program into the Calculator" if you need more detail.

Enter the program as described here.

Instruction	Explanation
:Input "A?",A	Causes the program to display the prompt **A?** and then to store the value the user enters as variable *A*. Press PRGM, use the right arrow to highlight the **I/O** menu heading, and press ENTER to select **1:Input**. Enter **"A?",A** (using the ALPHA key for all but the comma) and then press ENTER.
:Input "B?",B	Enter as described previously.
:Input "C?",C	
:√(B2-4AC)→D	Evaluates the portion of the formula that involves the square root and assigns this value to the variable *D*. (The value within parentheses is known as the discriminant.) Use the x^2 key to get the exponent 2 and the STO> key to get the →.
:Disp (-B+D)/(2A)	Displays the answer that involves adding the value of the radical expression. Find **Disp** as you did **Input**, under the **I/O** menu after pressing PRGM. Be sure to use the negative key, (-), for the negative symbol in front of *B*.
:Disp (-B-D)/(2A)	Displays the answer that involves subtracting the value of the radical expression. Enter as described previously.

Press 2ND [QUIT] to exit the editing mode. To run your program, position your cursor on an empty line on the home screen, press PRGM, highlight your program on the **EXEC** menu, and press ENTER. When your program name appears on the home screen, press ENTER again. Enter the coefficients when prompted to do so, pressing ENTER after each one.

```
PrgmQUAD
A?1
B?8
C?-12
           1.291502622
          -9.291502622
                  Done
```

www.ingramcontent.com/pod-product-compliance
Lightning Source LLC
LaVergne TN
LVHW081316060426
835509LV00015B/1548